John Morgan

A Vindication of his Public Character in the Station of

Director-General

Of the Military Hospitals, and Physician in Chief to the American Army

John Morgan

A Vindication of his Public Character in the Station of Director-General
Of the Military Hospitals, and Physician in Chief to the American Army

ISBN/EAN: 9783337173364

Printed in Europe, USA, Canada, Australia, Japan

Cover: Foto ©ninafisch / pixelio.de

More available books at **www.hansebooks.com**

DIRECTOR-GENERAL

OF THE

MILITARY HOSPITALS,

AND

PHYSICIAN IN-CHIEF

TO THE

AMERICAN ARMY;

ANNO, 1776.

By JOHN MORGAN, M. D. F. R. S.
PROFESSOR of the Theory and Practice of
PHYSICK in the College of PHILADELPHIA;
Member of several Royal Colleges and Academies,
and Philosophical and Literary Societies, in EUROPE
and AMERICA.

TO THE HONORABLE

...GRESS of the United-States
... AMERICA,

...ery FRIEND and WELL-WISHER
...he RIGHTS and LIBERTIES of MANKIND,

THE FOLLOWING

...NDICATION

...HIS PUBLIC CHARACTER,

...tation of DIRECTOR-GENERAL
...E MILITARY HOSPITALS,

...HYSICIAN in CHIEF
THE AMERICAN ARMY,

IS,

...deference to Rank and Authority,
WITH ALL BECOMING FREEDOM,

...RFULLY SUBMITTED

B Y

...R MOST RESPECTFUL
AND MOST OBEDIENT
HUMBLE SERVANT,

THAT a mean and *invidious* set of men have looked upon my elevation to the rank of DIRECTOR GENERAL AND PHYSICIAN IN CHIEF, with an *evil eye*, and long been concerting *my removal*, is a matter of which I have too substantial proof to doubt: That the unwearied pains I have taken to support œconomy, regularity and order, so far as they had been introduced into the department, before it came under my management; to introduce, recommend and inforce them, where wanting; and to oppose and reform abuses that were creeping, or had already crept into it, from the infancy of the service, were the root of the enmity which sprung up against my proceedings, are no less certain. It is equally evident that it received its growth and vigour from my inflexible resolution of being faithful to my trust, in not suffering so far as it was in my power to prevent, the dissipation of the stores entrusted to me, for the uses of the sick that should be sent to the General Hospital under my care, by exposing them to the waste and depredation of m. whose schemes tended to the subversion of the General Hospital, in which they laboured to raise themselves in an importance, which neither the General nor Congress ever intended, and from my putting a stop to those abuses of which too many of them had been guilty. That these are the stock from whence have shooted those clamours, against me, which have been so carefully cultivated, with a design to injure my character with the publick, under a pretence of interesting them in the sufferings of the sick, to which the imprudences of others had given rise; and to shift the blame from them on me, I doubt not will appear to the full conviction of every impartial person, who has patience to attend to the following Letters, Narrative, Proofs and Illustration of facts, which I propose to lay before them.

But

But that my enemies should be able, with all the arts of malice, to have influenced Congress to proceed to my dismission, on their partial reports, is what I had no thoughts they would have been so bold, or so base, as to attempt; nor if they had, could I have imagined that they would have succeeded in their attempt.

The manner in which I have conducted myself in the General Hospital department; my strict observance of the resolves of Congress; my vigilance, care and activity in the duties of my station; the several plans I devised for putting it in the power of Congress, consistently with their own original schemes of œconomy, to make a better provision for the rigimental Surgeons and sick, as well as for the General Hospital itself; the advices I have communicated from time to time to several of the members, concerning the state and wants of the sick, and of the regimental Surgeons; the evils I have foretold were likely to ensue, and the remedies I pointed out in time to prevent many of them; and lastly, the toils and dangers to which I have continually exposed myself in discharge of my trust, I concluded would always be a sufficient shield to protect me from every assault, till I could have notice of the designs and movements of my enemies, been prepared for my defence and have had time to have repelled them. Those instances of zeal diligence and uprightness of conduct, I hoped, were such, as neither malice could scandalize, nor envy misintrepret.

Will it be believed in a future day, that so grave and illustrious a set of men, as compose the American Congress, should, on any partial representation, without giving the person accused an opportunity of exculpating himself from the charges brought against him, or knowing what he was accused of; and without calling on him to offer what he had to say, why he should not be so dealt with; making themselves judges as well as hearers, pass sentence, as if all that is said, is proved? Will it be believed then, on no better evidence than the clameurs mours and misrepresentations of interested men, they would have dismissed, from an office of the greatest trust, One, whose established character and their good opinion had called from private life, and exalted to that station; One, who, nevertheless, from his first stepping forth on the stage of action, had always met with public approbation and distinguished honours, both at home and abroad; who had served his country in posts of eminent trust and usefulness, with applause; that they would, on the first application, have sacrificed him to the crys of a faction? Would such a proceeding be thought consistent with equity, or been compatible with the reputation of a less important Assembly? Would it be thought an act of common justice, in such a court, to proceed to punishment, on a charge, which might be groundless, and that, for ought they knew, might have been refuted, as soon as mentioned? Are the Members of Congress well assured, that on a *mere pretence* of something being done that ought not to have been done, or something being omitted that ought to be done, they have not made a victim of an innocent, or even meritorious servant, to promote the ambition of an INDIVIDUAL, or cover the faults of MANY, as if that offering would make atonement for their oversights or misconduct? Is the dismission from an office of such consequence, a matter of so little moment, as to stand in no need of even the formality of an inquiry? Can such a step reflect honour on the most dignified Body of Men in America? Is nothing further necessary to find a person guilty, than to accuse him of being so? Could that Assembly be certain, that they were not, by this proceeding, invalidating their own resolves, weakening the obedience due to their commands, and shaking the very foundations of their authority?

To degrade an officer from his rank, however lightly it may be thought of by vulgar minds, is an act of the highest rigour, as it opens the mouth of obloquy, and points the tongue of slander with deadly venom.

What

What reparation can be made for such a hasty judgment, if it is found to be so? Can any future inquiry into the merits of the cause wholly extinguish its fatal influence? Is there a tribunal in the world that has past sentence without a trial, that one may pronounce a proper tribunal, to which an innocent man may safely appeal? The higher the tribunal, the more fatal is the influence of prejudices. Has not the part the Congress has taken, in my dismission, a direct tendency to weaken and corrupt the proper evidences? Can witnesses that might be called in be so impartial, as to give a full and faithful testimony in favour of the accused person? Will they readily produce such proofs in his favour as they could do, that might tend to applaud his conduct; whom Congress, by a resolve, has thought fit to censure, especially when those witness have their reliance on that Court, for present rank and future promotions? Is there a more effectual bribe to stop the mouths of evidences in favour of an innocent man, and to raise up enemies against him? How unhappy then must be the situation of any one, which lays him under so great an inconvenience, that those who have it in their power to justify his conduct, may be intimidated from doing it, fully and freely, as they wish to do, for fear of giving offence to those on whom they are dependants; so that it is easier for those who incline to it, to do an innocent person a mischief, than to find many men so just, as to produce all they know in his behalf, and, by vindicating him, incur the disfavour of those in power?

Under those circumstances a man's defence must be liable to misconstructions; whereas, had an inquiry been allowed, before dismission, full weight would have been given to the evidences on both sides; but by this summary and unusual proceeding, is not the door shut against impartial justice; and should the person be called to trial, before the Bench that condemned him, are not his Judges become a party against him? In whose favour they are likely to pass judgment, on reference, let the feelings of mankind determine! Notwithstanding

Notwithstanding I was fully sensible of the force of these reasonings, yet so conscious was I of my innocence, and such was my opinion of the incorruptibility of the Congress, that, rather than lay under an imputation that affected my character, dearer to an honest man than life itself, on the first notice of my removal from office, I immediately appealed to the Commander in Chief and to Congress, in hopes they would reconsider what had been so hastily done against me. Three months are elapsed since that appeal, nor have they thought fit to give me any answer.

To what other cause can I impute it but their own reflexions, that there is not a set of men on earth, so free from the influence of their own passions, that a person may trust himself to their decisions, unheard, and to whom it is proper to appeal from their own decisions thus made? For who are so free from bias, as not to have a secret wish to find, that, in passing judgment, they were just. Can it be their desire to find that man blameless, to whom they have behaved, as if they thought him otherwise? Would it not be a reflexion on their hasty judgment, when they have treated him, as guilty, to find him wholly innocent?

But I will not do that Honourable Body the injustice to entertain a suspicion so derogatory to them, as to consider my dismission, and the manner of it, as a regular, deliberate act of the Whole Body, or what they approved. I have heard it alledged, in their defence against so injurious a supposition, that many of the most respectable Members were absent; that some of the States were not represented at the time; and that several of the Members were wholly oposed to it; that it was an act into which they were suddenly forced, by the clamours of a party, whom political necessity, at the time, compelled them to gratify.

But such is my opinion of the integrity, and such my reliance on the honour of the Congress, as to believe that when they are furnished with the materials for

judging

properly, they will be as ready to do me justice, as a part of them have been to listen to the malice and misrepresentation of my adversaries; and to shew their magnanimity, by allowing that they have been capable of an error, by their readiness to redress it. These considerations have induced me to print such an account of my proceedings, a may enable them, and the publick, to see with clearness, and judge with conviction, on the propriety or impropriety of my conduct; and to put it in their power to condemn, or acquit me, on sufficient evidence.

To suppose, as some have been inclined to think, that Congress can object to this appeal, from their judgment, to that of the publick, would be a greater reflexion, in my opinion, on their justice, and do more injury to that veneration we are bound to pay their virtue and wisdom, than I think any Advocate of Liberty will dare to offer so respectable a Senate Would it not be incompatible with every idea of that liberty and justice for which America is now in arms, to dis-allow an honest freedom of defence and expostulation, or to shut up the channels of communicating intelligence, by which the publick may be truly informed of the propriety of their proceedings, if they mean to maintain the confidence of those who have surrendered to them their power and rights, not for their own, but the public good? Without this is allowed all our priviledges are but an empty boast, "*the baseless fabrick of a vision,*" to which we are sacrificing the most substantial realities.

Out of respect to Congress, I have thus long deferred my application to the publick. I can no longer, consistently with my reputation, defer it. The wounds that are given by the envenomed tongue of calumny are deeper, and more fatal than the sword; they destroy what is dearer than life, reputation and peace of mind; blemishes on a man's public character soon fester, and if not speedily removed, will contaminate every thing about him, and infect the very air he breathes. He whose reputation is injured, is ever fufpected; his fociety is fhunned; he is looked upon as dangerous, as a walking peftilence. I muft not therefore pafs over, in filence, a proceeding which ftrikes fo home at my honour. It would afford room for ingenious architects to raife a pile of plaufible charges, which filence is no ways calculated to refute. Evil reports are apt to fpread like wild fire, and even perfons not eafily inclined to it, by repeating and circulating a ftory fnow ball it from hand to hand, whence it cannot fail to accumulate; and where flanders have been fuffered to take root, there are never wanting fome perfons, who will ufe all kinds of manure to quicken the growth. And though my Friends are difpofed to look upon me as an innocent and injured perfon, yet I do not defire that they, or the world, fhould fet down fatisfied with a bare prefumption of my innocence, as my enemies have with that of my guilt. I rather wifh them to unite, in calling on me; to perfift in dragging from their dark retreats, and chaining down thofe barking CERBERI, thofe pefts of fociety, who lay in wait to prey on the reputation of others; and to proceed in laying open my conduct, and their evil machinations, fo long as any doubt remains of either, and the means of obtaining and communicating evidence on the facts, are within my power.

Before I enter upon the tafk, may I be permitted, without offence, to guard againft a miftake that fome may, perhaps, otherwife fall into. They may fuppofe, from the pains I am taking to vindicate myfelf from groundlefs imputations, that I wifh, or aim to be reftored to the place from which I have been removed; and that I ought rather, on the firft appearance of the injuftice done me, to have refigned my commiffion, by which I might have freed myfelf from much trouble, and have avoided the public difcredit of being removed from it. After I have given fuch evidence, as I have done, of the readinefs with which I confented to ferve my Country, at the firft call, as a proof of my principles, and of my

obedience

obedience to their commands, I flatter myself I may, without offence, be allowed to acquaint the world, that, on the very first intimation I ever received of the complaints made to Congress, I called for an immediate hearing. The honourable Member who informed me of them, gave me a hint of resignation being the most adviseable step to be taken, in the like circumstances, to quiet those clamours. Could I have first vindicated my innocence, I should have resigned with pleasure, for I had not the remotest wish to continue in an office that was so intolerably burdensome, when there was such want of discipline to inforce those regulations, which both the Congress and Commander in Chief thought were best; nor did I think a service that, for want of discipline and suitable provision, was in a state of the utmost anarchy and confusion, so very honourable, as to have a desire to remain in it, one moment longer, than by so doing I could be useful to my Country.—But had I resigned, before I had been favoured with an examination into my conduct, it might rather have prepossessed the world with an opinion, that there was some ground for those clamours against me, of which I was no ways conscious. I determined, therefore, to insist on an inquiry into my conduct, and having fully vindicated it, to have closed with their permission to resign, had it been allowed me to do so.

I should then have rejoiced to have escaped from that scene of confusion to which I had been so long a witness, and in which I could not be useful, to my former station, in private life. On this ground I consider my dismission, not only as more honourable than a resignation, without a previous justification of my conduct, but than a continuance in office, under the circumstances I have been in, almost ever since I accepted that commission. But I particularly rejoice in it, as it affords me an opportunity of vindicating my conduct, not only to the Whole Congress, but to the Whole World, and

having

having done it, I leave the event to that God who rules the world, and in whose hands are all our ways.

Every thing I deem necessary, at present, for my full justification, is contained in the following letter to a friend at Philadelphia, my memorial to General Washington, and the letters and resolves of Congress, with the proofs and illustrations that are subjoined in the appendix. I shall make no other apology for laying them before the publick in that form and order, than that I think them the best adapted to give both Congress, and the publick, full information of the nature of my conduct; and if, in the course of my narrative, the facts I adduce, and the remarks which arise upon them, should seem to glance obliquely on any particulars, I hope I may be allowed to plead that the treatment I have met with, and the nature of my vindication, requires freedom, and that I shall be excused in the eye of reason, and with every candid mind, if I do not smother the truth, and thereby weaken my defence, merely to avoid giving pain to any.

A LETTER to a friend at Philadelphia.

Boston, April 17, 1777.

"*Pudet hæc opprobria nobis,*
"*Aut dici potuisse, aut non potuisse refelli.*"

Dear Sir,

I Am obliged to you, for the accounts I have received of those loud clamours, which have been circulating through Philadelphia, at my expence. I have inclosed, and already sent to the post-office, the news-papers of last week, and of this day, containing my answer to those injurious charges so groundlessly, and yet so maliciously propagated, by certain virulent caluminators, which, I flatter myself, will open a door for a full and ample vindication of the whole of my conduct; a conduct which I shall never suffer to be traduced, in so
vile

vile a manner, as hath been attempted, by a set of weak, or designing men, whilst I have a tongue to speak, or a pen and hand to employ, to clear myself from those aspersions.* It

* The news-papers, here referred to, are the Independent Chronicle, of April 10th and 17, and the Boston Weekly Advertiser, of the 17th; from which it may be proper to acquaint the reader, that in that of April the 10th, being informed of some evil minded persons who had taken upon them to raise and circulate a number of false reports and groundless clamours, at Boston, on account of my having taken possession of the medicines and shop furniture of Dr. Sylvester Gardner, and Dr. William Perkins, of Boston, for the use of the army; and to alledge that many of the sufferings of the sick, in the last campaign, arose from my having unjustly with held from them (or from the REGIMENTAL SURGEONS) those stores which they were entitled to draw from the General Hospital, I came to Boston on purpose to call upon the persons pointed out, as the principal authors of those reports, requiring them to make good that charge, and at the same time inviting any persons, who had any thing to offer against me, that regarded the faithful discharge of my trust, to step forth, and state their accusations. I then promised to lay before the publick, a faithful and exact account of every proceeding, relative to the discharge of my duty in the above station, by which the world would be enabled to judge whether the charges were well founded, or only proceeded from a spirit of malignity and detraction.

In the papers of the 17th, I communicated the result of that examination, with a letter, calling upon the author of the report, concerning the removal of the medicines, to know what he had to offer; to which he returned a short evasive answer, disclaiming the charge, which is there published, together with a full account of the transaction.

In that paper the public were informed, that in respect to the removal of the drugs, medicines and shop furniture in question, I had the order of General Washington, in writing, for what I did, backed with a resolve of the Council and Assembly of the State of Massachusetts-Bay, after a sequestration of the property of those persons;—that they were removed to New-York, for the use of the army,—that whatever was done by me, in this affair, was merely official;—that an inventory of the whole was left with the Boston Committee, that in case the former owners should return to town, and be entitled to claim a restitution of their effects, the value might be duly ascertained;—that a particular and faithful account of every thing done in this business, was transmitted to the Adjutant General, to be laid before the Commander in Chief, for which I received thanks for the matter and manner of what I had done;—and that an inventory of every hospital store, remaining on hand, being made out by the Apothecary of the General Hospital, with care and exactness, was transmitted to General Washington and the Congress, of which I kept an authentic copy; concluding this head with an address to those persons, to take shame and confusion of face to themselves, who, judging only from the corruption of their own hearts, appear to think it impossible for men, to whom much is entrusted, to keep free from that pollution of hands, which they find in themselves such a proneness to contract.

In regard to the second charge, which relates to the with-holding the hospital stores; this being reported against me, by Dr. Story, Surgeon of Col. Little's Regiment,

It is in vain for any of my friends to expect, that I will set still under the base imputations, or rest satisfied in that general perswasion they all have of my innocence, or acquiesce in any thing short of a full and impartial discussion of every particular, relative to my proceedings, in my late station.

You would comfort me with this true observation, that "it is not for men in public stations, in times like these,

regiment, I wrote a letter to him, April 8th, calling on him to explain himself for taking such unwarrantable licence as he had done, assuring him that no man, be his rank in life what it may, should be suffered to do it, with impunity; Dr. Story declining to take any notice of it, that letter was published in the Independent Chronicle, of the 17th of April, with the following Declaration of Col. Joseph Trumbull, Esq; Commissary-General of the American army.

To all whom it may concern.

BE it known, that—whereas I have been informed that it has been industriously propagated by some evil-minded persons, in divers parts of the Country,—That Dr. JOHN MORGAN, late Director-General of the Continental Hospital, has drawn from the Commissary-General's office, the well rations, for the sick, while in the General Hospital, and that he has pocketed the same for his own emolument; I have this day made examination of my books, clerks, &c.— and find that I have not a charge in my books, of A SINGLE PENNY paid to said Doctor MORGAN, or any other Hospital Surgeon under him, on account of rations for the sick; nor did I ever PAY any thing, on that account, to Doctor MORGAN, so that there cannot be the least foundation for such aspersion of his character.—I have paid LARGE SUMS for the rations of the sick, in *Regimental and Brigade Hospitals*, to many Brigade and Regimental Physicians and Surgeons, but never a farthing to said Doctor MORGAN, or any General Hospital Physician or Surgeon whatever.

Given under my hand at Hartford, 2d of April, 1777.

JOSEPH TRUMBULL, Commissary-General.

N. B. *The publick are now informed, that Dr. Story having afterwards insinuated —that, " when he was properly called upon, he did not doubt he should be able to support what he had at any time advanced." I called upon him in person, for an explanation, when he thought fit to deny, that, at the very time he affirmed the sufferings of the sick to have arisen from the cause assigned, of withholding from the Regimental Surgeons or sick, what he supposed them entitled to draw from the General Hospital; (to which, however, they had no claim) " he had any thought of Dr. Morgan's having any intention to defraud the Continent." Lastly, it is proper it should be known that the aforementioned invitation, if any man had any thing to alledge against the faithful discharge of his trust, to step forth and declare it, has been also printed in the Rhode-Island, Connecticut and Philadelphia papers, without any the least reply; from whence all men may judge how groundless, as well as malicious, those clamours were; and, no doubt, will, in behalf of injured innocence, feel a just indignation at the authors thereof.*

to expect to be free from censure, nor should they be discouraged at the obloquies, with which some men wish to stain their characters; they ought to content themselves with this remark, that men of worth, who are not only innocent, but whose conduct is meritorious, are most liable to be traduced by ignorant and designing men; that not *to meet with envy* and *back-biting*, is a *frequent effect* of *compliances*, which argue a *weakness* unworthy of *confidence*; that my friends know I do not wish to be *popular* at such a *price*, but have rather courted the slanders of the *envious*, by a steady perseverance in my duty, than lay a train for the compliments of *flatterers*, by favouring their *dark purposes*."

You proceed in remarking, "That it is no unusual matter, in the want of success in any undertaking, for those who have been the authors of any public calamity, in order to shift the fault from themselves, to lay it at the door of others."

You say you are convinced, that what I wrote to you of my suspicions, was true; "that this cry against me is owing to my steadiness to discharge the trust reposed in me, according to the best of my judgment, knowledge and abilities, and in not yielding to the repeated attempts of ignorant or bad men, to encroach upon my department, who wished that I would issue all expensive stores to their orders, without their being accountable for them, contrary to my instructions, by which they would be exposed to rapine and dissipation, without a possibility of replacing them, and my character justly suffer for submitting to an unlicensed prodigality and breach of duty and orders. You observe that mine "is not the only instance of a man's reputation being offered up a victim to the ignorance or ambition of others."

You tell me you now see clearly, what I had often told you before, and have now experienced to my cost:" That it is no easy matter for a person, placed at the head of any department, that requires a strict and wary attention, not to be borne down by ignorant or designing men,

men, or to preferve the dignity of the place committed to him, without which however, he muft unavoidably expofe himfelf to a thoufand rude attempts to difhonour his judgment, and oblige him to act inconfiftent with it." You wifh me to fupport myfelf under this reflexion, that, "the beft provifion thofe men can make, for all events, who are above fuch compliances with the ways of the world, as may impeach their honour, or offer violence to their confcience ; and to whom the judgment and approbation of the world is matter of but fecond confideration, is to have a firm confidence in Providence, that he will not fuffer their innocency to be utterly oppreffed, or notorioufly defamed, and yet expect the gufts and ftorms of rumor, envy and detraction ; to look on thefe as a *purgatory* he is unavoidably to pafs through, and depend upon time, and the goodnefs of heaven for a vindication ; and by conftantly performing all the duties of his place and ftation with juftice and integrity, prove to all men, how groundlefs thefe charges were, that men of fecret defigns have imputed to him."

To thefe judicious reflexions and obfervations, permit me to reply--That to pafs over, in filence, a proceeding, which ftrikes fo home at a man's reputation, as that of his difmiffion from a public ftation, and being fuperceded, without a caufe affigned, will be confidered, by moft of mankind, as an argument of confcious guilt.— The complaints which have been made, ought furely to have been heard before a court of war, which was doubtlefs the proper method of proceeding for offences, fuppofed to be committed againft the army, before which fuch an inquiry might be made, as would determine the validity of the accufation, and how far the perfon accufed was worthy of condemnation, acquital, on honourable acknowledgments of the fervices he had done, and particularly for his care to avoid all thofe methods and precedents, which men of lefs fcruple would have laid hold of, for their own advantage, and thought even juftifiable. Is it not hard to meet with fuch treatment as this, when a person's conduct has been highly meritorious, in the sacrifices he has made by entering into the service; the loss he has endured in it; the fatigues, toils and dangers to which he has been exposed; the throwing himself out of business, and making himself a marked character to serve his Country, in a post wherein his countrymen conceived he could be particularly useful, from his former experience and knowledge in military hospitals, when they could meet with none other who had the same pretence to experience, that would accept of it; and who has suggested, to them the proper plans for improving and putting it on a better footing than he found it? Must he, in silence, behold others run away with the merits of his performances and build on his foundations, who could neither pretend to the same experience, nor done the same duty nor run the same risks and hazards, and quietly put up with the misplaced censures of the publick? Must he content himself with the repeated "*sic vos non vobis*" of the Mantuan Bard?

Where is the honour of a service, or what the safety of accepting a place of trust, if the most punctual compliance with the orders of his superiors, and in many instances, contrary to his own judgment, is to lay the foundation of a man's ruin? If any subtle malicious or vindictive INSINUATIONS, on the one hand; or the AMBITION of aspiring men, on the other; shall, at any time, prevail against those, who have made a sacrifice of their private interests, to follow their Country's call, in their particular station; who value their integrity more than popularity, and cannot be brought to act in contradiction to their conscience or judgment, however powerful attempts are made to oblige them to do it; or if the character and reputation of one, who has served the publick, in places of rank and trust, faithfully, irreproachably, with honour and applause, is to be immolated to the MISREPRESENTATIONS of others, or to the designs and wishes of a more SWELLING INTEREST, without any trial, or giving the party accused the least notice

notice of what nature were the complaints laid to his charge, or who were his accusers, that he might be able to show to the world, how groundless the accusations were, and how far their clamours were founded on private pique, disappointed expectations, or secret resentment?

Does not this conduct tend to overthrow the foundation of civil Liberty, which can only be secured by impartial trials, before dis-interested Judges, where the accused person and the accusers, are brought face to face, and where full weight is given to the evidence in favour of the accused? What line is there betwixt this and DESPOTISM? At this rate, who is free from the fatal effects of influence? Have not the States of America claimed this essential right, as one of the main pillars of their Liberties? Or have Americans, who contend against what they declare to be an illegal usurpation from abroad, on the natural rights of mankind, no laws to secure them from oppression at home? Has the British subject a defence against that of a King, that should attempt to violate those rights, and an American none against the injustice of his equals, when joined with power to injure him?

Is it a misfortune, easily to be borne, that any persons should lay under a charge, which it was the duty of those, who are the authors of it, to have made good? Is it not consistent with the principles of equity, that every *accused person* should be deemed *innocent*, or judgment be suspended till guilt is proved? Let all consider, what mischief may happen to themselves, if, upon a general charge, without the mention of any one crime, a person is to be degraded from his rank and office; for who is secure from the consequences of such a precedent? Or, if men of secret designs can thus shelter themselves, by sacrificing those, who, from a sense of duty, remain immoveable against every effort to draw them aside from their duty, who is certain that he shall escape the danger?

To

To INCAPACITATE, in this manner, is no such small punishment, that a man may easily endure, though he be innocent. "It is to SCOURGE; it is to WHIP with SCORPIONS; *it is a punishment calculated only for* GENEROUS MINDS, *thus to rob men of their* HONOURS;" it is to lay a stain upon them, which, though undeserved, a whole life is too short to efface the impression, without it be fully vindicated; and, to them, is worse than death. It reaches to innocent friends and relatives, who would rather hear of their death, than their disgrace. It is to destroy a man's peace of mind; it is to expose him to the tongue of slander, and the rude attempts of wicked men, who, by their behaviour, seem to think it a merit to load him with reproaches, as one without the shadow of a virtue,

"*Nulla virtute redemptum*
"*a vitiis.*"

But if I am proved guilty of misconduct in my office, let my guilt meet with its desert; but on me, on me alone, let the public indignation fall: Let not one friend ever pity me: Let every trace of sympathy and compassion be obliterated from the tender breast of every relative; of every dear and tender connexion! On the other hand, if I am found innocent, I must insist upon my right, of publickly asserting and maintaining that innocence, although hosts of evil-minded men should oppose themselves to the attempt, and I trust in Heaven, that it will come forth, on the test, as gold tried in the furnace, without mixture of alloy.

Nor shall I rest, at ease, till my vindication is as well known, and circulated as far as the malice of my accusers has spread, and the disreputation fully wiped away, which the Congress has cast upon me, by so shameful a dismission from office, on a mere accusation, without proof, and without an hearing, although repeatedly called for before that took place; and I apprehend it will be found, upon proper inquiry, that at the risk of my reputation, so grosly and shamefully insulted, and of popular favour,

favour, which I might easily have acquired however, at the *trifling expence of honour, and of the trust reposed in me by Congress,* whilst I was fighting in their cause, having escaped the secret ambushes or latent enemies. I was placed, Uriah-like, in the forefront of battle, amidst enemies set in formidable array against me; then deserted, and left to fall, unsupported, by those who placed me there ; and whose duty it was to have protected me

If one, who being only accountable, by his commission, to the Congress and Commander in Chief, and who was more particularly under their wing, could not be sheltered, *even by them,* from so furious an onset, such a violation of the common rights of mankind, till he could be brought to trial, and his guilt or innocence established on undeniable evidence, I ask, once more, who then is safe ?

You have gone on, Sir, to tell me, " that on the first rumour of my dismission, and the manner in which it first took place, you felt all that indignation that might be expected from friendship, on so interesting an occasion ; but that you suffered but a few moments of reflection to take place before you were convinced of the falsity of the charges which you say, you are sure I can clear up to the entire satisfaction of an impartial world ; as you proceed, you enter into the sensibilities of my own heart on the first news of my being treated so unworthily."

As you discover a desire to know what reception these rumours met with from myself, I must inform you of certain circumstances that prepared me, in some sort, to think that ill offices had been done me, by unknown persons; which I was determined, if possible, to find out. I acknowledge that I felt resentment rising in my breast, on occasion thereof, the first emotions of which I could not suppress ; I was resolved to restrain them, however, till I had set on foot an inquiry into the causes of such treatment, as I met with, and, if matters were not explained to my satisfaction, to resign my commission, and bid adieu to a service, in which an injury was offered to my sense of honour.

By the votes of Congress, October the 9th, it seems I was, in effect, degraded from the rank of Director-General and Physician in Chief, to the rank of Director only, and restricted to the department on the East side of Hudson's-River;—whilst the Director of the flying camp, who had been appointed, after the campaign began, to the temporary service of that campaign, without waiting the issue of his services, was put on an equal, or, to say the truth, a preferable footing, contrary to the rules and discipline of war * Instead of making his reports to me, as Director-General, as had been formerly ordered, by a Resolve of Congress, July 17, we were both to make our reports to Congress. I was ordered to establish an Hospital, at a proper distance from camp, for the army posted on the East side of the North-River, when there was no convenience for doing it on that side, at any suitable distance, being hemmed in by the two rivers, and the enemy's forces, on either side. He was to establish an Hospital in the Jerseys, on the West of Hudson's-River, and to direct it, where alone any suitable accommodations could be provided for the sick, with any the least regard to the convenience of the army, or the preservation of the sick. Here almost the whole of the Hospital stores and medicines were lodged, and near one half of the Hospital Surgeons and Mates of my department were; as well as all the wounded brought from Long-Island, and the sick of the General Hospital at New-York,

---

* That I might not mistake, I wrote to Mr. Gerry, a Member of Congress, for an explanation of that resolve: His answer is as follows.

Philadelphia, November 20, 1776.

"I have received your favour of the 7th instant. With respect to the meaning of the resolve of ordering the "DIRECTORS" to take care of the sick, as they may be on the East or West side of the river; it appears to me to be this, that whatever sick of the army shall happen to be on the East side, they shall be under the care of yourself; and the others under direction of Dr. SHIPPEN."

I am well informed, by a gentleman of unquestionable honour and veracity, and who had seen his letter to Dr. SHIPPEN, about the same time, that his address to him was, to Dr. SHIPPEN, "Director-General, &c." "A word to the wife."

New-York, who, as the object of my peculiar care, were conveyed to the Jersies, for their greater safety and better accommodation.

At this very juncture, it was the General's pleasure that I should proceed to Hackinsack, on the West side of the river, to establish other hospitals for the increasing sick. I applied to him, to know in what light I was to consider those resolves; and whether, consistently with them, I could continue to establish hospitals, or provide for the sick that should be carried from the East to the West side of the river, so that they should remain under my own care and superintendence, or whether I was not, by those resolves, to be deprived of the only hospitals I had, that were fit for the accommodation of the sick and wounded, and of the principal hospital stores which I had left, that I could command; they being, at the retreat from New-York, sent to Newark, the only place, where they could be dispensed with safety and convenience, for the use of the troops on New-York island, and in its neighbourhood.

But General Washington and General Green, who was present, gave it as their opinion, that the resolves of Congress extended only to distinguish the two armies, for which separate hospitals were to be established; that I was directed to establish one for the sick and wounded of General Washington's army, that was posted on the East side of Hudson's-River; and that the other gentleman was to take care of the sick of the flying camp, and such other of the troops, as happened to be then on the East side of the North-River, which was only a temporary station. This view of matters, in some measure, composed my apprehensions at that time. I was unwilling to admit the supposition that Congress, which, I was bound to think, wished order and subordination to be kept up in every department of the army, intended that he should interfere with my power, and superior appointment of Director-General, though, for the sake of present convenience, he might be ordered to

make

make his report directly to Congress. I therefore concluded, as well from the construction put upon it by the Generals, as from the reasonableness of the thing itself, that I was not prohibited from fixing hospitals, either on the east or west side of the river, as best answered for the army posted on the east side. I could not conceive that the lives of the men, that composed that army, were to be sacrificed, by a limitation of the place in which they were to be taken care of, or that a plan was laid for reducing me to a mere cypher, and to throw the whole power of the department into the hands of an inferior officer, as Doctor Shippen certainly was, however he might affect an equality.

Agreeable to this inference, I repaired to Hackinsack, by the General's order, to direct the necessary provision to be made, for the reception and accommodation of the sick, from York island, and directed a second division of the Hospital Surgeons, of my immediate department, to attend, and take the care of them.

Although I never was allowed to be absent from the army, and scarcely permitted to be at any distance, for the shortest time, from Head-Quarters; yet the great weight of providing for, and taking care of the sick of the whole army, rested on my shoulders alone; and yet my hands were so tied up by resolves of Congress, and general orders, as to leave little freedom for proper exertions. In particular, I had no Deputy or Assistant under me, to share any part of the burden of my department, however extensive. One Surgeon and five Mates were all that had been allowed me, from the beginning to this time, for every five thousand men; when at least one thousand men, in every five, were sometimes considered as unfit for duty. And though I was called upon, as if I was a Commissary, to attend to the daily provision returns of all the sick in the army, spread thro' many miles, not only of the hospital, but the regimental sick, and to provide them with accommodations, as a Barrack-Master, and with hospital furniture, as a Quarter-Master, and

and that, contrary to the resolves of Congress (so ignorant and unreasonable were the Regimental Surgeons, and even some of the militia Generals, in requiring it) yet I had no other aid, than what could be afforded me by those gentlemen, who had only the rank and pay of Hospital Surgeons, but who were obliged to do the duty of Deputy Directors, for which I wished them to be cloathed with more power, than they were entitled to, when acting under the simple commission of Surgeons.

Perhaps artful men may here alledge, that I ought, therefore, to have submitted to the difficulty, and discharged my care of the sick, of the army, on the western Director. I would ask them for what purpose, whether to bury him with the load, when he could no more take care of the sick of the flying camp only, than I could of the whole army, unless by depriving me of my own officers and stores; or was it, to reduce me to a cypher, in order to raise him into importance? Had the Congress supposed that I had too much, and he too little to do, I would cheerfully have transferred to him the superintendence, and management of as many, as his heart desired, only reserving my rank, and the command of my own officers, hospitals and stores. But I have good grounds to believe, that his underhand attempts to interfere with me, in my department, and his interest with a particular set, which has been employed to effect my removal, with a view to promote his design of succeeding me, have operated more powerfully to accomplish it, than all others, that have been held up, as the ostensible causes of my removal; which, however he may think, from being transacted behind a curtain, they lye concealed, can be easily traced to their author, and are of a tissue with the rest of his conduct towards me, on similar occasions.

But whilst I was left destitute of help, what assistance was allowed, in the mean while, to the Director of the flying camp? I was well assured, from his own lips, that he had not long acted in that station, before he was
complimented

complimented with the appointment of a deputy, having the rank, title and pay of Assistant-Director, or, as he told me, however strange and inconsistent it may appear, of Assistant-Director-General. Thus it fares with the man, I will not say as Haman did, whom the king delights to honour; but whom governing connexions chuse to make considerable, at the expence of others.

However this was effected, whether by his own forecast, or that of his friends, will any man pretend to say that this appointment, and the manner of wording the resolves of Congress, October 9th, did not serve the purposes of nest eggs, on which to brood and hatch designs, not thought of by Congress, as a body? What will indifferent men think of these resolves, so contrary to my commission of Director-General, October 17, 1775, and the report of Congress, August 20th, to establish my rank beyond dispute? See the appendix, page 30.

Whilst such an auxiliary appointment is made to give weight and importance to a temporary Director of a flying camp; and resolves procured afterwards, to raise him to greater importance, and to bring me down to a level; and when subsequent measures are taken, to dispossess me of the powers of action, to tye up my hands, and yet to make me accountable for misfortunes, beyond human reach to prevent, and for the misconduct of others; to transfer my stores, my hospitals, my surgeons and officers, to another; and yet blame me for the consequences: who is so blind as to see no designs in all this, or so wilful, as to ascribe the whole to mere accident? Is it not manifest, that the Director and his attachments, have, from his first coming into the service, pursued such measures, as they conceived were best calculated to raise him over the shoulders of every man, who stood in his way, and to constitute him Head of the department. How truly Machiavelian has been his conduct, and those who have assisted him, *per fas atque nefas*, to accomplish his ends, whether right or wrong, to make

D all

all things subservient to them; "to couzen and deceive, so long as it answered any purpose, and might contribute to what he desired upon motives, how foreign so ever; and when that failed further to serve his purposes, to compell submission, by force, to what persons are not able to oppose? How consistent is such conduct with such principles? Where men have entertained designs, that are void of all conscience, they must not think to prosecute them, by the rules of conscience, which was laid aside, or subdued, before they entered upon them; and must make no scruple of doing all those things, which are necessary to compass that, to which they have devoted themselves."* I am persuaded, that both he, and his adherents, have not only watched for, but made occasions, to serve as a plausible pretext, for displacing me, to accomplish their own wishes. I am not more assuredly convinced of my own existence, than I am fully persuaded, that had any other person been Director of the flying camp, and were it not for that object, no clamours of the sufferings of the sick, which were trumpeted through every State, nor any other charge of mismanagement, would have been laid at my door; or that I should have had an opportunity given me of being heard in my defence, and that my conduct would have been fully vindicated, and my reputation for diligence and fidelity, in the discharge of my trust, have been established, beyond the reach of calumny.

That I may not seem to advance this, without a reason, I shall not place the whole stress of the argument upon the single circumstance of no particular charge being ever made known to me, by Congress, although I repeatedly applied to know what was the accusation, and who were my accusers, and no other person was ever called upon, in the department, none accused, or sought after, as if I was answerable, not only for every supposed crime that could be alledged against any part of it, but for mere misfortunes; on which I have been proceeded against, and treated in a manner, that, I believe, has no precedent: I

---

* Machiavel's political principles.

shall

shall produce such circumstances, as, I trust, will convince impartial men, that the ostensible causes of my dismission, were not the true ones; and that Congress had, in fact, no well grounded charge, to justify the measure, which some persons were so resolutely bent upon, as to be afraid, if I were admitted to an hearing, their designs, of effecting my removal, would have been frustrated. I think the one I have already pointed out will be found, on an impartial inquiry, to be the *conditio sine qua non*; or rather, the efficient cause of that event; I mean that I stood in the way of an ambitious man, whom his adherents determined, be the consequences what they might, to raise to the first rank in the department, and either oblige me to bend, as a reed, before him, or, like a stubborn oak, to be torn up by the roots, for resisting the tempest; and to plant him on my ruin.

I had intimations given me, more than once, that pains would be taken, to deprive me of my rank and distinction, to make room for a rising competitor. I did not readily believe, yet did not wholly discredit the intelligence. I wrote to some members of Congress, whom I looked upon as my friends, to guard against any step, which, through seeming inattention to military rules, might make it impracticable, consistent with those rules, as a man of spirit, to remain in the service. I told them I did not seek for any extent of power, nor was I averse to any limitation of it, in my own case, compatible with that sense of honour, which is supposed necessary to actuate and quicken men, in every army. I did not know, till I received a letter from the Secretary of Congress, to rectify that mistake, that rank, precedence and honour, are all nonsense, and not looked for in our army; and truly, if we may judge from effects, they carry too much conviction, that a sense of honour is no virtue, in his estimation, whatever it may be in that of some men, of a more liberal way of thinking, both in Congress and in the army. I took the liberty to write to the President of the Congress, himself, " that I hoped there would be no unnecessary abridgement of rank and authority in my person, whilst I continued in office, that was necessary for the head of the department, in the person of my predecessor, and was consistent with real usefulness, to which I expressed it to be my desire, that every other consideration should give way, as it would imply a reflexion upon me, which I was unwilling to suppose I merited."

I also wrote to the Secretary of Congress, on a double account; first, to know the extent of my power, and that of the several Directors, for the sake of conducting business in its proper channel; and next, to get that rank, which was allowed me by Congress, properly recognized by the several Directors, to avoid mistakes. Dr. Stringer, one of the Directors, had not only disputed it with me, and refused to make his returns to me, as Director-General, as Congress required; but appealed to Congress for its decision, which was given in my favour. *See appendix, page 30.*

Although my application to him was respectful, and as I informed him, only made with a view to know my station, and that of others, that I might perform the duties expected of me, without interference with any; instead of favouring me with any extract from the resolves of Congress, to which I referred for information, he saw fit to substitute his own dictates, in place of those of Congress. See page 149, 150, &c.

My rank and authority being securely fenced in, by repeated acts and resolves of Congress, there was no possibility for the Director of the flying camp, or his friends, to accomplish their secret purposes, without first breaking down the separating wall of distinction. By this means, the person, who would not submit to be degraded from his rank, would be obliged to resign, and, to insure success, it was easy for artful persons to excite or encourage complaints, and to bring them before Congress, to afford a pretext for displacing him. But then it was of consequence, that he should be kept ignorant

...count of those complaints, and of his accusers, and to prevent his obtaining an hearing, lest he should vindicate himself, and thereby disappoint their hopes. Nothing could answer their purposes better, than to push for obtaining his dismission, without a trial, which might enable him to clear himself from all aspersions, and justify his conduct in the face of Day, to the confusion of his enemies.

After this detail of facts, compared with the several resolves of Congress, and the proceedings thereon, with the relation I am about to give of the particular behaviour of the Director, in consequence of them; let every impartial man lay his hand upon his heart, and ask himself, ingenuously, what he thinks of the whole matter, and of the several appearances, which concur, in an uniform series to point to one object? Will they view the resolves of October 9th, and the manner of wording them, after all that had passed, as a mere accidental mode of expression, in men so wise, so much accustomed to weigh, and so well acquainted with the import of words and the force of language, and as only intended to re-iterate, and renew former appointments, without any design, in those who framed the resolve, I will not say to throw dust in the eyes of the Members of Congress, in general, but to draw them into a measure, of which they might not consider its tendency, not only of effecting an alteration in one department, but of making such an entire innovation upon another, as was not generally thought of, and would lead to the great changes that have since taken place?

Can it be said that neither the Secretary, who, though no Member of Congress, has an interest with many of them, without doors; nor any of the members themselves, were apprized of the difficulties that would, unavoidably, arise from a resolve of Congress, calculated to throw down the former settled distinctions, of July 17, 1775, and 1776, and August 20, last; in which my rank was so clearly recognized and established. One part of my errand

errand to Philadelphia, laſt June, was to confer with the Committee of Congreſs, on the neceſſary eſtabliſhments for keeping up a clear and regular ſubordination in the General Hoſpital, through all its various departments, and this was the ſubject of ſeveral letters, to different Members. If any of the Members of Congreſs had diſcovered, in me, any want of abilities, for ſo important a poſt; is it not reaſonable to imagine they would have openly, and avowedly, aſſigned it as a cauſe of diſqualification? But did they ever do it? Nay; what ſays the Secretary, himſelf, in his letter, of Auguſt 14, by way of making ſome acknowledgment for the miſtake he had committed, in his former, of Auguſt 2d. It is the teſtimony, not of a friend, but an enemy, and one, whom I believe to be a deep agent in my removal. I will therefore quote his very words; for "*fas eſt ab hoſte doceri.*"

"There is no man, Sir, acquainted with you, who can doubt of your abilities. All the world bears witneſs of them, and the learned in Europe, who muſt be allowed to be the beſt judges, have given ample teſtimony, by the honours they have heaped upon you. While you exerciſe your great talents, for the benefit of thoſe entruſted to your care, your Country will honour you, and poſterity will do you juſtice; even though Dr. S——, when you chance to meet, ſhould refuſe to give you precedence."

I proceed to the relation of what happened, in conſequence of thoſe reſolves of Congreſs, of October 9th, and the ſtrange behaviour of Dr. Shippen, the weſtern Director, thereupon.

Being at Hackinſack, ſoon after this "*new arangement,*" as he was pleaſed to ſtile it, took place, I employed myſelf, with all poſſible induſtry, to put the hoſpital affairs in ſuch a train, at Hackinſack, that Dr. Warren might conduct them, without my preſence afterwards, that I might, without hinderance, be able to proceed to the White Plains, to which place, General Waſhington,

and

and the army under him, had marched, a day or two before; and the British troops were taking the same rout. I called, therefore, on General Green, at his camp, near Fort-Lee, to represent to him the situation of the sick, at Hackinsack, and to request his orders for procuring Dr. Warren such assistance, from the Quarter-Master-General's, and the Commissarial departments, as he required. I met the western Director there, who, with a peculiar freedom, becoming the elevation to which he seemed to consider himself as already raised, or to be raised, demanded why I was not at my post, on the other side the river? Accustomed to receive accounts from others, and to give orders myself, in the affairs of my department, I cou'd not but feel the indignity of being thus taken to talk by him; and answered him accordingly. I discovered his desires and aims, but concluded he had more LEE-WAY yet to make, than to entitle him to avow his sentiments so openly; but in this, it seems, I was mistaken.

The day following, Dr. Foster, to whose charge I had left the direction of the hospital, and care of the hospital stores, at Newark, came over, in haste, and desired a private conversation with me, on a subject of some delicacy. As I had visited Newark, within a very few days, and every thing was reported to me to be in good order, and I had left all the directions I thought necessary for future regulations, previous to my return to Head Quarters, I could not conceive the occasion of this unexpected visit. But my foreboding mind took the alarm, of which I was yet ignorant of the cause for he informed me it was of such a nature as made him think it improper to communicate, by letter.

After this preparation, he informed me, that the Director had called on him, and proposed, but with great art and address, the surrendering up of the hospitals and stores to his Direction; the care of the sick to remain under the same persons whom I had sent from my department, but to act under his authority. He replied that he considered himself as under my direction only, in hospital matters; and that he did not think himself at liberty to deliver up the stores to any person, without a written order from General Washington, or the Director-General. To this the Director made answer, that whatever like, or dislike, I might shew to this proposal, I should find myself obliged to acquiesce in it.

The construction which the gentleman put upon this proceeding, was, that the appointment of the Director, being, to form and superintend the hospital of the flying camp, would terminate in a little time, as the troops, composing the army, raised for that service, were enlisted but for a few months, unless he could carve out some place that he could be pleased with, in the mean while, that would put him on a better establishment. I commended his prudence, in declining to deliver up the stores, without proper orders, and desired, that, if any further demands, of the like kind, were made by Dr. Shippen, to refer him to me, for an answer.

The Director had expressed himself to me, about a month before, in a manner that corresponded with the above idea. He told me, frankly, that he should like, well enough, to continue in the service, as he thought it a more gentlemanny life, than that of a drudging private practitioner. I was truly desirous of his continuance in that station, if he could remain in it, without elbowing me out of any thing that appertained to my place; for I did not then imagine he had yet aspired to the place itself.

Having served in the army, the whole of last war, and had pretensions, on that account, to some years experience in military hospitals, which he knew nothing of; and having been appointed to the chief direction of the hospitals, the preceeding year, and having borne the burden of the day, ever since, it had not yet entered into my imagination, that I was soon to give place to the very man, who, but four months before, not four months, nay, scarcely three, had written to announce

his

his appointment, as Director of the hospital of the flying camp and that he had enlisted himself in the service of the American States, confessed his being a mere novice in the management of his (subordinate) department, and applied to me for instructions in the *etiquette*, the word by which he chose to express his notion, of the government of a General Hospital; and who promised, from time to time to report to me the state of the hospitals under him, agreeable to an order of Congress for the purpose; but which, however, he never did. Perhaps he judged, from better information than I could ever obtain, that so soon as he had learned the "*etiquette*" of military hospitals, his elevation would render it unnecessary.

But what surprized me, in his late conduct, was, that having an opportunity to acquaint me, the day before, in person, at General Green's, with his expectations and demands on the hospitals I had established, he did not chuse to say any thing to myself on the subject, but to apply to subordinate officers, to accomplish his wishes, rather than treat with me as a principal; I thought this portended no good; but then I knew it was of a piece with very many other instances of his conduct, on different occasions.

I went over, in a day or two after, to the White-Plains. A letter soon arrived from the Director to General Washington, complaining that his situation was uneasy, for he could not obtain the command of the stores at Newark, and of course of the hospitals I had established there, and of the officers I had detached from my particular department, unless by the General's orders for the purpose, or by directions from me; for which, however, as I observed before, he had never applied.

The General was pleased to communicate this letter to me. I represented to him the inconveniences of depriving me of those stores, and that I had no others, in any sufficient quantity, to answer the continual calls

upon me; that the reft of the ftores, which, at his command, were ordered to Stamford, (and from thence were removed by the Stamford Committee, without my knowledge, and with his approbation, as I afterwards learned) could be of no ufe to me, at that time; that the only medicines, which could be got at, were thofe at Newark, which I had fnatched as a brand out of the fire, at the retreat from New-York; and that I had appointed an Apothecary on purpofe to affort and difpenfe them out to Regimental Surgeons at Newark, as there was no poffibility of doing it in an army, conftantly moving from place to place, under all the inconveniences we fuffered. To be borne down, with inceffant demands from all quarters, was hard indeed; and to be deprived of the only refources I had left me, thofe of my own providing, and of my own faving, with extreme difficulty and hazard, to be at the fole command of another, a junior, and inferior officer, appeared to me to be an unreafonable demand. I had, already, detached near one half of the Surgeons and Mates, of the General Hofpital, to Newark and Hackinfack, and by the General's command, eftablifhed hofpitals there, at the very time I had forefeen out the probable confequences that would enfue from the extraordinary refolves of Congrefs October 9th. There were, at this time, above fifteen hundred fick, at thofe two places, under the care of my own Surgeons. I had juft received letters from them, which fhewed they were gradually working through all their former difficulties, by fteadily purfuing the directions I had left them: With thefe advantages and their own experience, they were more likely to compleat the work, than they would be, if in the midft of it they were to receive new directions from one, who, with all due deference to his abilities, was lefs acquainted, than themfelves, with the arrangements of a General Hofpital. I obferved, that to deliver up the hofpitals, ftores and officers, would be to ftrip me of all power of being ufeful; and it was not
in

in the power of the director to supply their places, if the stores, hospitals and sick, were to be committed to his care, and my proper officers were to return under my command, on the east side of the River; whence the sick must suffer; and if the stores were delivered up, we ourselves must become destitute and helpless, and yet exposed to greater clamours than ever. I had, in no instance, interfered with the Director of the Flying Camp, but offered to give him every assistance in my power, that he was pleased to call for. But to be stripped of the rank of a Director-General, and the power of my station, and to be left but the shadow of a Director, and yet to be accountable for every accident, or misconduct of others, as well as of my own department, and, from the highest post, to be rendered the mere dependent of a junior and subordinate officer, was what I never would submit to. Sooner than be subject to such controul, or give up the stores and hospitals, which by the General's orders I had established for the sick of his own army, when I had no convenience for providing others, I would give up my commission.

The General promised he would, and I doubt not but he did write to the Director, in answer to his letter, "That the hospitals I had established, and the surgeons and stores I had sent to Newark and Hackinsack, were to remain under my direction."

What was my surprize to hear, after some time, from some of the officers of the hospital that were under me, in the Jerseys, [for it seemed proper that I should never know, but in a circuitous manner, what most immediately regarded myself,] that those stores which had been provided for General Washington's army, and which I had saved at New-York, and sent to the Jerseys for safety, and for the convenience of issuing out to the hospital sick, under my own care, and to the Regimental Surgeons, were now actually ordered, by a late vote of Congress, to be delivered up to the Director of the Flying-Camp; and that he received letters, at

this

this very time, from some of the Members of Congress, addressed to him by the title of William Shippen, Esq; Director-General of the Hospitals, &c. of which I took notice before. Whether this too could be mere accident, or an unintentional, unmeaning compliment, time will soon, I believe, reveal *

My Clerk, some time after this, but before my dismission, produced me an order, in Doctor Shippen's hand-writing, formally demanding an exact list and surrender of all the hospital stores that did belong to me, and which were in his possession, as if I were already degraded from my rank. What is more, Mr. John Adams, a Member of Congress, I am told, above a month before, actually called on Dr. Foster, with whom I had left the care of all my stores, advising, or counselling him to deliver up the stores to Dr. Shippen; but in all this transaction, I never had one line from any of them, to that purpose; on the contrary, Mr. Gerry gave it as his opinion, in the letter he wrote to me, that the stores and officers were to remain under my own direction only.

When I found it necessary, for the good of the service, to deliver up a part of my medicinal and hospital stores, to one of Dr. Shippen's surgeons; he refused, till repeatedly required, to give any other receipt for the delivery of those stores, so insolently demanded, than one which carryed insult in the stile of it; and the demeanour of most of his officers at Bethlehem, when I was there, was that of men who knew my dismission to be pre-determined, and looked upon themselves therefore as authorized, by the example of their superior, and justified for dispensing with every call of good breeding, if ever they had any. *Quid faciant Domini, audent cum talia Fures?*

Whilst I was fixed by the General's order, at the lines, near the White-Plains; Fort Washington, Fort Lee,

* Doctor Shippen, since writing the above, is appointed to my place of Director-General and Physician in Chief.

Lee, Hackinfack, Newark and Brunfwick, fell into the hands of General Howe. In the mean time I procured from Boston, to which place I had sent exprefs, as well as to Newport, Rhode-Ifland, Providence and Norwich, and from Hartford in Connecticut, by the affiftance of Governor Trumbull, a frefh fupply of medicines and hofpital ftores. I appointed hofpitals at Stamford and Norwalk, and Surgeons from the General Hofpital to receive and take care of the fick and wounded: I went in perfon to both places: Near two thoufand men were received into them: Not a fingle one was refufed: They were well taken care of: The greater part of them recovered: All clamours and complaints on that fide, ceafed; they were only heard in the weftern department, where the fick fpread through the Jerfeys, Pennfylvania and Maryland, in a tract of 200 miles, amounting to near one half of the army; Thefe fell under the care of the Director of the Flying Camp; but he was unequal to the tafk, and retired to Bethlehem, with a fmall handful of fick; and the deficiencies of his department, over which I had no controul, were afcribed to me. As if, unaffifted by any deputy, or proper aids, I was in my own perfon, to go through all the drudgery, alone. Had I the eyes of an Argus, their vigilance would have been infufficient, or had I the hundred hands of a Briareus, I could not, of myfelf, have performed all the labour that was required, to be accountable for the defects of others, burdened with fo great a charge, whilft all proper fubordination was wholly difregarded.

Being anxious, however, to give what affiftance I was able to General Wafhington, and the troops which had croffed over to the Jerfeys, I followed them, fo foon as I had taken the proper fteps for providing hofpitals at North-Caftle, and Peek's-Kill, for the troops left in thofe places, and haftened to join General Wafhington. I croffed the Delaware, and reached Head-Quarters juft as the enemy came in fight, at Trenton. I waited on his Excellency, and thus, with the respect due to the Commander in Chief, but with firmness, addressed him: "Sir, I know not in what light you will think proper to view my haftening to what I efteem my duty, an attendance upon you, without waiting for your commands. Your Excellency will permit me to acquaint you, that from the nature of my commission, I am appointed to direct the hofpitals for the army under your command (I have a letter from the Secretary of the Congrefs, with thefe words: " the department at Head-Quarters, is under your immediate direction.") To be reftricted then to the eaft fide of the River, is contrary to my original appointment, on which I accepted a commission, and unlefs I am reftored to my rank and place, wherever you command in perfon, I muft give up my charge. I cannot confent to this degradation from my rank and authority. If this is the return I am to expect for my toils, fatigue and fervices, to be obliged to make way for a new officer, whofe intereft and rifing favour, like Aaron's rod, are to fwallow up every confideration, it is time for me to leave the army: And to thefe difficulties am I reduced, in confequence of the refolve of October 9th, without I receive a farther and fatisfactory explanation." The General was pleafed to reply in the following words, as exactly as I can remember them: I hope, Sir, you do not imagine it is owing to me: I am here, without any affiftance from the hofpital department. In cafe of need, I know of no-body here to take the direction: I think it is very ftrange; I would have you lay this matter before Congrefs, that fome fteps may be taken to remedy this irregularity and inconvenience, and that I may know what I have to depend upon.

When, therefore, by permiffion of General Wafhington, I waited on Congrefs, for an explanation of their former refolves, which appeared to require it, and for farther inftructions, at a time when the liberties of America

rica appeared on the point of being swallowed up for ever, if some vigorous measures were not immediately pursued to apply an effectual remedy; and I had ventured, without waiting for orders, to fly to the place of danger, where I thought my presence most wanted, I had no doubts that I should no sooner have mentioned my apprehended grievance, than I should have had immediate redress. Fully persuaded that my services and sacrifices merited consideration, and entirely ignorant that malice had yet attempted to discolour the merit of my proceedings, I did not suspect that any crime had been laid to my charge, till I complained of the injury done me. So short sighted are mortals, and so true it is that a man is never exposed to greater hazards than when he least apprehends them. Now, for the first time, I heard of the clamours about the sufferings of the sick in the Jersies, and at Philadelphia; and although I had been restricted to the east side of Hudson's-River, to make way for one of rising interest, the misfortunes of the department committed to his care, were wholly ascribed to me, notwithstanding the direction was taken out of my hands, for his sake.

I applied for admission to Congress; Mr. Samuel Adams appeared. On mentioning the cause of my application, he gave me to understand that complaints were brought against me, and the sufferings of the sick charged to me, with circumstances greatly reflecting on my humanity. I denied the justice of the charge, and being at the door of the chamber where the Congress were setting, I thus addressed him: Sir, I do solemnly deny the charge, and do intreat I may this instant, be introduced to Congress, that I may have an opportunity of vindicating myself against every injurious aspersion. Of this, Sir, I am confident, the more my conduct, in the station of Director-General, is examined into the more lustre will it reflect upon me. I ask for an inquiry. I desire to know the particulars of the charge and who are my accusers, to meet them face to face, and am willing to stand the test of the strictest scrutiny.

I was refused admission, it being said the Congress was engaged in some important matter. I again desired the gentleman to inform me what particulars were laid to my charge? I could neither learn them, nor who were my accusers. As I could not obtain an audience, at that time, I begged Mr. Adams to inform Congress of the design of my coming, and my desire of admission, and I let him know that I waited at my lodgings, in expectation of an hearing, when Congress had leisure to grant it. I obtained it not. Congress adjourned to Maryland, without taking the least notice of my appeal to them. I repeated my application, through the same gentleman, by letter. My dismission took place without an hearing, and without any answer, and without suspending me from office, till they could be satisfied of the facts alledged against me; for this, it seems would be too great a condescension.

I would fain ask, whether such a denial of my humble request, and keeping me in ignorance of my reputed crimes, and secret accusers, is agreeable to humanity, or what is usually allowed to the greatest criminals? Is it a way to beget a reliance on the safety and honour of the House, that after having passed judgment, without an hearing, I may still depend on ample justice, candour and generosity of treatment? Is such a proceeding usual? Might I not have rather expected to have been first suspended, then tried, and judgment to follow, and not precede conviction, on any breach of order or misconduct?

Had I been conscious of guilt, may it not be presumed I should have sought to shelter myself, by a resignation, rather than insist on a trial? Could a better pretext have been afforded? The Congress, contrary to every known rule, by a resolve of theirs, had reduced me from the rank of Director-General, removed me from my right, of attending the army under the Commander in Chief to give place to a temporary Director, who, before, was made accountable to me, as head of the department;

clamours

clamours were raised against me, (groundless indeed!) I asked for an hearing, and was refused. Resignation was intimated to me, as what alone would quiet those clamours. What temptation was there for a person, conscious of guilt, to wish a continuance in office, till his conduct could be examined into? On the contrary, every thing was to be apprehended under that circumstance. The most imminent danger that the cause itself was lost filled the minds of many. I saw the black clouds gathering on the margin of the political horison, threatening, on every side, to over-whelm its abettors in a general destruction, on one hand; and myself in private ruin, on the other, unless I could make my retreat from the approaching tempest. Did I, cowardlike, basely fly; nay, the very appearance of danger determined me to face the storm, and prove the falsity of the charges against me. I met two of the Georgia Delegates. I acquainted them with what had happened; that I would stand by the cause, during the present dangerous onset; but when that was over, I would insist on an immediate hearing, and, if not granted, then resign.

I repaired to the scene of danger, but was ordered to the east side of Hudson's-River. Submission was my duty, for the present moment; redress my hope and expectation, so soon as Congress had leisure, and was in a situation to attend to it. I pursued my business, as though I had received no cause of complaint, till I could obtain an hearing. But instead of redress, the first account I received, but through an indirect channel, was that of my dismission. I had prepared, in haste, a narrative of my proceedings, in the department committed to me. I immediately sent it to the General, with a desire of its being laid before Congress, for their reconsideration of what was done, as I thought with precipitancy, and did not doubt that, on better information, they would quickly retract from the measure, or, at least, give me an audience, and judge on the evidence of facts, compared with their own Resolves, and the General's orders. At

At any rate, if they were determined to deliver me up to the cries of a faction, I thought Congress, for its own sake, would have let me down gently. If the sacrifice must be made to gratify it, I thought Congress would suppose that something was due to the character I had sustained in life, to the rank I had held in my profession, to the general reputation which public honours from the learned societies in Europe are supposed to confer. Upon occasion of such unworthy treatment as I have met with, I flatter myself, a man may be allowed to speak the truth, in his own favour, without an impeachment of vanity. I thought some consideration would have been had for that devotion of my best abilities, which I had shewn such as they are to the improvement of liberal arts and sciences in this new world; some regard manifested to an early and zealous attachment to the cause of American liberty; to the sacrifice I had made of my private interest and safety; to my own station, and that of some of my nearest relations and friends, both in and out of Congress, and of the army. And could not all these procure some shadow of levity, where a victim was to be offered up; something like compassion; some answer to my humble memorial, in my vindication, and my petition only "*to be heard*"? I must say none. Three months are nearly elapsed, whilst I have not received one line or message in answer. In the mean while as if that refusal was the signal; the alarm spread; news-papers bear witness to my degradation. Base and malicious men the pests of every society, have given free vent to their slanders. Boston has been filled with clamours to my prejudice. Villains there are in every place, to coin and circulate reports prejudicial to a man's character. But why should I pretend to enumerate the evil consequences of such a severity of conduct towards me? If it would have answered any valuable purpose; if the sacrifice of my life would have saved my Country, I could have chearfully offered it up. I shall not say so of my honour.

To

To the impartial publick I therefore mean to appeal. At this tribunal, no innocent person need fear to make his defence, nor to allow free scope to be given to that defence; where a man's conduct, and the motives of it being known, he has reason to hope for a candid judgment, free from prejudice or party. If I can but obtain this indulgence, I hope to evince, to every common understanding, the rectitude of my conduct, and if the most laborious and steady application to the discharge of my trust, and perseverance in the path of duty, can give a claim to hope, I flatter myself, that I shall not only escape their censure, but meet with the warmest approbation of the publick, which it ever has been, and whatever may be the success, ever shall be my study to obtain.

I am, my dear friend, theirs,

and your most devoted, humble servant,

JOHN MORGAN.

To his Excellency
GENERAL WASHINGTON,
Commander in Chief of the American Army.

The MEMORIAL and REPRESENTATION of Doctor JOHN MORGAN, respecting his Care of the Sick, and Manner of conducting the Department of the General Hospital committed to his Care.

SIR,

WHEN I was called by the choice of my country, to the station of Director-General of the hospital and Physician in chief, I left a respectable and lucrative practice against the judgment of some considerable persons in my native city, who, from regard to me, and what they conceived to be my interest, endeavoured in vain to dissuade me from accepting the post, truly honourable as they allowed it to be. Their advice had no influence over me. Without hesitation, I sacrificed it, with every future prospect of better expectations from continuing with them to the satisfaction of serving my country, AT THE HEAD OF THE HOSPITAL, IN THE ARMY, UNDER YOUR EXCELLENCY'S IMMEDIATE COMMAND.

Having had some experience, in times past, of the nature of the department, I have, ever since I took charge of it, made it my constant study, to make myself master of the subject, and to acquire a thorough insight into it. With what success, I do not think can be judged off, from the outside appearances of last campaign, and the causes which prevented the several regulations I proposed, from taking place agreeable to my wishes. It would be tedious to enumerate them all; yet it cannot be amiss to point at some of the principal. (*a*) The

(*a*) See the Appendix.

A

The first of these which I shall mention was, the want of sufficient time and opportunity before the opening of the campaign, to have all the regimental Surgeons properly furnished by Congress, and made acquainted with their duty, of which many of them were very ignorant, and the *error* of having them look to the General hospital for those supplies of medicines and instruments, &c. which it would have been better to have sent to them by Continental Druggists, who might have the means of collecting and preparing every article in a suitable manner, which it is vain to attempt in a moving army. Another cause was the want of a sufficient number of certain hospital officers and assistants, and the means of procuring them when allowed by Congress, which was late, as Commissaries, Storekeepers, Stewards, Ward-Masters, &c. (*b*) This difficulty was increased from the nature of the campaign, in which, contrary to expectation, it became necessary, to shift the places of the General hospital frequently, and to branch it out in such a number of hospitals widely distant from each other. (*c*) To these may be added, first, the want of sufficient help from other departments, which it was impossible to remedy in the state our army then was. (*d*)

2dly, The neglect of the regimental Surgeons, to report the sick of their regiments in season, and in an orderly manner to the General hospital, though often required in General orders, Resolves of Congress and otherwise, to do it; (*e*) and sometimes keeping back their sick from entering into it at all, or till they became very numerous; then discharging them all at once into the General hospital, at the time of an engagement with the enemy, and when the attention of the whole body of hospital Surgeons was necessary to take care of the wounded. And lastly, the frequent and long absence of the regimental Surgeons from their regiments, who, instead of sending the sick, as they ought to have done, to the General hospital, had them conveyed to some remote regimental hospitals, where they neither had, nor could obtain suitable necessaries for their provision and care. (*f*) On

On my first arrival at Cambridge, I set about to establish rules for the General hospital Surgeons. I had heard of many abuses being practised by enormous drafts of expensive stores from the General hospital, to which, with your Excellency's approbation, to whom I made report thereof, I put a stop and limited the demands of regimental Surgeons to such articles, as Indian meal, oatmeal, rice, barley, molasses, and the like, and required that such sick as wanted others, should be sent to the General hospital, that these things might be dispensed out under my own direction. (*g*)

The next reformation I attempted was to call upon all the Mates in the hospital to undergo an examination of their abilities, in order to select from the number those who were best qualified for the service.—This was followed by your Excellency's orders, to see that all the regimental Surgeons and Mates should pass a like examination. I began the task, but the movements of the army, the aversion of Surgeons to undergo these examinations, from which too they were often screened by their Colonels, and by pretence of sickness, &c. and the increasing business on hand prevented my proceeding far in it. (*h*)

When the army lay before Boston, the small-pox frequently made it's appearance in it, owing to the number of persons who came out of that city with the infection upon them, which endangered the spreading of the contagion amongst our troops. By the establishment of the small-pox hospital in a suitable place, with proper persons to take care of the sick, and the precaution of sending all infected persons to it, so soon as known to have the disease, and to cut off all communication betwixt it and the troops, the army was preserved from ever receiving any injury from it.

When the troops marched from Cambridge for New-York, all the sick were left behind in the General hospital, amounting to upwards of three hundred men. In less than six weeks, during which time but few died, I was able to discharge the hospital of every man, to settle and pay every accounts insomuch as never to have had any further demands from that quarter.

During this time, with little or no expence to the public but for package and transportation I collected medicines, furniture and hospital stores, worth many thousand pounds, and sent them on to New-York. The like quantity, I apprehend, could not be procured in any part of America. Nor were these obtained for the use of the army, without much trouble and affiduity, owing to a strong opposition that was made to prevent it. (*k*)——— Besides these, I was able, by means of the subaltern officers in the hospital, some of whom I employed continually at the work, likewise to collect to the amount of near two thousand rugs and blankets, near as many bedsacks and pillows which were taken up from docks, and were gathered from hospitals and barracks, &c. These being washed and aired served the last campaign when none others could be got, and many of them are yet in good preservation.—— At New-York I collected some hundred sheets, fracture boxes, and other useful articles.

It may be thought perhaps that I place a higher value upon these acquisitions than they merit; be that as it may, I am persuaded the like could not be obtained now for much less than thirty thousand dollars, which is equal to the whole amount of what I have ever drawn or expended for the General hospital, in the space of a twelve-month, including the pay of all the officers and all the hospital expences of every kind, which have fallen within my department to settle, and for the faithful expenditure of the same, I am ready to produce my accounts, receipts and vouchers, whenever called upon for a settlement. Yet the General hospital has had the constant charge of a number from two or three hundred to a thousand sick and upwards to provide for and attend. Nor have any articles of the public stores been embezzled or mis-applied, nor the sick suffered in the General hospital for want of any thing I thought them entitled to draw from the hospital, and that I could procure for them. The

The medicines and stores provided, as abovementioned, have been appropriated with equal faithfulness and strict œconomy to the use of the General hospital; or issued from thence to regimental Surgeons, or remain on hand, subject to your Excellency's order. I have never burdened the Quarter-Master-General's department with any unnecessary demand from thence. And as to the Commissary-General, he will do me justice, as he has often declared himself on that head, that my drafts were within the most reasonable bounds. I am persuaded that of the sick who have been drawn for in the General hospital, if none of them have been drawn for at the same time with the well men in their regiments, the stoppage of their rations will go a great way towards paying the whole of the expences the hospital has been put to, on their account, for provision and stores of whatever kind. (*l*)

In a conference I once had with your Excellency at Cambridge, on the subject of hospital expences, you told me, and I took it as a hint of caution and advice to observe the strictest œconomy in my department (from which I have never deviated) that you were fearful the expences of the General hospital would exceed the estimate that had been made of them, by a person of experience in General hospital matters. If I rightly recollect, your Excellency thought the sum mentioned to be ten thousand pounds sterling per annum. I was surprized, and concluded the gentleman was mistaken; I resolved however, if possible, to employ such strict œconomy in the department, as to keep within those bounds, yet was fearful it could not be accomplished, on account of the advanced price of every article of living and hospital stores. Desirous of knowing what were the principles on which he founded the calculation, I wrote to the person that was mentioned, on the subject, in answer to which he informed me, that the estimate, he had given in to General Gates was ten thousand pounds sterling, for every ten thousand men, for six months, and so in proportion, which is equal to 40,000 £. ster. per. annum, for 20,000 men, the number then kept on foot. At

At the same time, as one qualified to give me full information, I wrote to him with a view to clear up all doubts, or to confirm my sentiments in regard to the manner in which the regimental Surgeons were supplied in the British service, with medicines and instruments, and to know what right they had to draw stores from the General hospital; to which his answer corresponded with the opinion I had ever entertained of the nature of the service. 'Till Congress, or your Excellency should give orders for a different mode to be pursued, I considered myself to be bound in duty to keep the British establishment constantly in my eye, as a directory, making allowance for the nature and difference of the service. (m)

Moreover, I was afterwards favored with your Excellency's opinion on the subject, contained in those observations you was pleased to bestow on the plan of regulations, which, by your command I sketched out, for getting again into a proper train, after we had, by one accident or another, been forced from the original plan of a General hospital, and got into confusion, on account of the opposition, some of the resolves of Congress, of July 17 last, met with from many of the regimental Surgeons, and the impracticability of complying with others of them, in the situation we were then placed. Your words were, "What is the practise in this case in the British army? Why should we think of improving upon their system, founded on long experience?"

Upon first entering upon the duties of my station, apprehending that the General hospital was not amply supplied, as I could wish, with bandages, old linnen and other implements of surgery, that would be required, in case of an action, I set myself to supply those wants immediately, which I effected with little expence of money, but with great labor, in which I had all possible assistance from the hospital Surgeons and Mates. I collected large quantities of old linnen, lint and sheets, made up six thousand bandages, and six hundred tourniquets, for the use of the General hospital, &c. which, though sufficient for a present exeigency, I did not think more than might be wanted for six hospitals, which I managed at that time.

Being then desirous of knowing how the regimental Surgeons were supplied, I proposed the calling upon them in general orders, for that purpose, and with a view to learn whether their assistance could be depended upon in the field, and whether they were properly furnished with medicines. Except Mr. Magaw, Surgeon of Col. Thomson's regiment, and a few others, they had scarcely the shadow of a supply—I gave in a report thereof, with a weekly return of the sick; I also stated to your Excellency what I conceived to be my duty, and that it was limited to the care of the sick in the General hospital.

This inquiry into the wants of regimental Surgeons, made them turn, as it were, on the General hospital. They wished to furnish themselves from it, with those articles of dressings, which the hospital Surgeons had collected, and made up for themselves, which those gentlemen thought an unreasonable demand. Farther, the regimental Surgeons wanted, contrary to all usage, to draw from the General hospital, all they should call for, in the way of stores, whether diætetic or medicinal, for the use of the sick retained under their care, in regimental hospitals, and to be provided by me with instruments and bandages, or to fix the odium of their insufficiency at my door. I therefore recommended in my report the necessity of providing (not in the army or General hospital) but from Continental Druggists (for that was what I intended) " a capital set of medicines, instruments, &c. as soon as possible. and advised that portable chests should be furnished from every regiment for a whole year, at once, and each chest be provided with instruments and bandages."—I did not expect, weak handed as I was, with respect to officers and assistants in the General hospital, from its very establishment by Congress, that this task would be enjoined on me, I thought my duty pointed out by that establishment, as much as I

could

could well execute, and which only related to the General-hospital itself; although with an earnest desire of promoting the good of the service, I early pointed out the wants of the regimental Surgeons, and in time for having them supplied with necessaries after the manner that has always been practised in the British army. I wrote to inform your Excellency, "that my commission only extended to the care of the General Hospital; the plan of establishment by Congress, of July 28, 1775. The list, number and arrangement of officers, and my instructions from Congress, which were wholly silent concerning regiments, their Surgeons or supplies confirmed this opinion," not to say any thing of the low estimate, which I had understood was formed for the support of the General hospital.

I then gave it as my opinion, grounded on the custom of the British army, of supplying the medicine chests by stoppages, "that if the sick, remaining in regiments, were to be supplied at a public expence (and not by stoppages) that expence ought to be made a regimental charge, and might be delivered in with an abstract of the regiment, (or any other better way.) that the General hospital, having nothing to do with the affair from its very nature, ought not to be burdened with their supplies; for then, on the number of sick admitted in the General hospital being known, the expence necessary for their support could, after a while, be better estimated from experience."

I then called on your Excellency, in the same letter, "for instructions what to do?" I informed you "that the nature and design of the General hospital, being little understood, and the nature of my duty so much mistaken, both by the regimental Surgeons and officers, and many things expected from me, impossible to be complied with, I apprehended it to be absolutely necessary that certain regulations should be fixed upon, to ascertain my duty, and those of the Surgeons and officers under me, as well as those of the regimental Surgeons, which all

ought

ought to know, and not hospital and regimental Surgeons only, but in general, every officer of any rank in the army, to prevent interference and mistakes."—

Besides giving this information, in order to bring about a farther explanation of the matter, and with a view to accomplish the end proposed by it; when I came to New-York, I laid a plan before the regimental Surgeons, to ascertain their duty, with a draft for a memorial to be laid by them before Congress stating their present difficulties, of which they approved; and I wrote pressingly myself on the subject, to the Doctors Committee of Congress; and at various other times I have delivered my opinion on the duties of regimental Surgeons, which may be seen in the general orders, particularly of July 3d, and July 28th, 1776. But although the sentiments contained in those orders were enjoined by your Excellency to be made the rule of conduct, and I think they were well calculated to answer the purpose, yet they were little regarded by many of the regimental Surgeons, and openly opposed by others. (*n*)

With respect to the manner in which I came to have the charge of supplying all the regimental Surgeons with medicine chests, &c. contrary to what I had always conceived to be the proper method, or usual for a General hospital, as I had always declared, I beg leave to remark, that the surrender of Boston having put us in possession of a large, though unassorted stock of medicines, hospital furniture, &c. your Excellency was pleased to order me, by the Quarter-Master-General, to put up medicine chests for five regiments, at Boston, Salem and Marblehead, &c. about the time the rest of the army moved to New-York. This I cannot but look upon as the beginning of all my subsequent difficulties. When I arrived afterwards at New-York, your Excellency was at Philadelphia, and I was repeatedly called upon by letters, and in the way of personal applications from regimental Surgeons and officers, to furnish several regiments that were at New-York, and others gone to Canada, with

B medicine

medicine chests. My hope and expectation had been, that out of the whole stock I had collected, I might be permitted to take such as were wanted for the General Hospital, and then to deliver the remainder to any Commissary or Continental Druggist, appointed by Congress, or by your Excellency, to receive it, for the use of the public, and particularly for furnishing regimental Surgeons. I received several intimations at this time, from different persons, that Congress expected from me to supply the northern army with medicines and hospital stores.

Having received no orders, however, for that purpose and the campaign then opening, I thought it highly expedient to receive clear instructions on that head, and applied for leave to go to Philadelphia, to have a conference with some members of Congress to know what I had to depend upon. Your Excellency gave me leave of absence for ten days, and although it proved too short a time to settle the business of my department, yet I returned punctually on the day appointed.

Before my arrival at Philadelphia, I learned that the Congress had purchased a valuable stock of medicines, which were in the hands of some druggists in town, out of which (on a supposition I imagine that they had more than would be wanted for public use) such considerable sales had been made by permission of Congress, and large quantities sent to the Southward, that it appeared to me there was danger, from the great reduction that was made in it already left the best collection of medicines I had ever seen in America for an army, might slip out of the power of Congress from such sale, &c. which might prove a loss they might not have it in their power to retrieve in the whole year (o) I therefore presumed to caution the committee against it. Upon conferring with them on the subject as I had, though contrary to usage, been obliged to put up medicine chests for some regiments, I understood if I might be allowed such a share of what was on hand as might be wanting from time to time to assort

those

those in my possession, to use my best endeavours to supply regimental chests to the regiments at New-York under your Excellency's command, for one campaign by way of trial; for I did not want to shrink from any labor, assigned me, whether my proper duty or not, by which I might serve my country, as far as it was practicable for me to do it.

I did not conceive from all I was able to learn that there would be more than forty or fifty regiments assembled at New-York; nor did I suppose that one half of those would come destitute of medicines and chirurgical apparatus, when I heard that the Southward regiments were supplied by the Continental Druggists; and I had taken pains at Cambridge, occasionally, to acquaint General officers, Commanders of regiments and regimental Surgeons, with my idea that they were not to look to the General hospital for those supplies, but have their regiments furnished, where raised, as being the most easy and natural method; nor did I expect such numerous detachments of militia, all of which came unprovided, and looked to me for supplies of every thing they wanted, not chusing to send their sick to be under the care of the Surgeons of the hospital.

I supplied from 40 to 50 regiments with medicine chests by the end of August, besides all the branches of the General hospital at New-York in the bowry and neighbourhood, and on Long-Island, which reduced many of our capital articles to an insufficiency for the General hospital for the remaining part of the campaign. And these I was obliged to come by where as well as I could; for although there was a great show of medicines and furniture left, yet many of the principal medicines being exhausted, and other articles not being duly prepared, nor such as were usually called for or wanted for regimental use, that show availed but little. To give what were at hand and could be spared from hospital use, which the regimental Surgeons would neither accept of nor be answerable for, would be, as scripture expresses it, to give one that asked for bread, a stone; or for an egg, a serpent. It

It was by your Excellency's command that I shipped off part of the stores, as I did, to Stamford to prevent the w... e being lost, in case the enemy should possess themselves of New York. From thence they were sent into the country, as some frigates had got into the Sound, and it was easy to land near Stamford, whereby the stores might be destroyed. (*p*) It was by a like command that I visited Poppon, Haverstraw and Orange, to look out for a suitable place for a General hospital; and by your orders, in writing that I went over to Newark a day or two before the evacuation of New-York, to make provision for about a thousand sick includ... ose wounded at the last action on Long-Island, who were there committ... d... ... e of D... ... ... r... net, surgeon... he General hospital, with seven or eight Mates to take care of them. (*q*) Part of the medicines remaining at New-York, were ordered over by the Adjutant-General, to whose personal activity and the assistance he gave to the Surgeons, it is owing, that they were saved. The most valuable part, however, was still left in New-York, when the enemy had effected a landing, drawn a line across the island, and were supposed to be then entering New-York. (*r*)

At this critical juncture, I went over with some of the hospital officers and brought off all that had been left, in a pettiauger, which was filled therewith. I had ordered two chests, for hospital use, to be put up and sent to Kingsbridge, it being impossible to get more up there, in a retreat.

The sick and wounded above-mentioned were landed in haste and disorder, at Hobuck Wehock, &c. Some of our Mates fell into the hands of the enemy, and many of the Nurses and Waiters fled, and the militia ran off and impressed every waggon they could find in the neighbourhood. It therefore required some days to get on all the sick and wounded, through many difficulties, from the fright of the inhabitants, and their reluctance to admit of the hospitals being stationed at that place.

I had provisions to collect, a Commiffary and Ward-Mafter to feek, and Nurfes and Waiters to procure, with every thing neceffary for the comfortable accommodation of the fick and wounded. I had but little affiftance enough to perform this tafk, your Excellency having enjoined me to leave the moft confiderable number of Surgeons and Mates at York ifland, in cafe of need. I made all poffible hafte, however, to put the hofpitals at New-Ark on a fafe footing, which I accomplifhed in about ten days, and then returned to head-quarters.

After this, judge, Sir, of my diftrefs, to find how much this affair had been mifreprefented to your Excellency, as I perceived it was by a letter juft written to me by your Aid-de-Camp, fetting forth the miferable fituation to which the fick were reduced, and the clamour for want of medicines abfolutely infifting on an immediate and fufficient fupp'y. for " whilft I was referving the medicines for cafes of emergency, the fick were dying in numbers for want of a neceffary fupply." I had juft fent to an eminent private Druggeft, as well as to Mr. *William Smith*, the Continental Druggift, at Philadelphia, praying for a fupply of fuch articles as either I had not or could not be got at, enclofing each of them a lift for the purpofe (*f*) Inftead of ten pounds of Tartar Emetic, I fent for, four ounces were all I could obtain for the whole army, fcarcely equal to the demands of a fingle regimental Surgeon, or for one day's confumption for the army I prevailed on the Surgeon of a regiment to go exprefs to Hartford, Norwich, Providence, Rhode-Ifland and Bofton, to procure medicines which places were fo bare of the articles that we principally wanted, as to occafion a great difappointment. What is more worthy of remark, they never came to hand till a fhort while before the retreat from Hackenfack. I had applied to Governor *Trumbull* by letter, for fome affiftance, which, though it was fent as expeditioufly as poffible, took time. (*v*) I alfo applied in perfon to the State of New-York, at Fifh-Kills, hearing they had part of a ftock of medicines

purchafed

purchased for the use of that State on hand, and found it had been ordered to Albany for the use of the Northern department.

What made it more astonishing that the number and clamors of the sick should be so great at that time is, that in a consultation which your Excellency, General *Green* and General *Parsons* had, a few days before the evacuation of New-York, it was there proposed to send off the sick and all unfit for duty in brigades, with some careful officers out of each brigade to attend them, and money to defray the expences of suitable accommodations and refreshments; and a Surgeon was ordered along with the sick of each brigade, that they might not suffer for want of medical assistance. (*w*) I am still of opinion, it was the best step that could have been taken to prevent the sick from falling into the enemy's hands, unless what I once mentioned to your Excellency as my wish could have been accomplished, viz. That protections might be granted to the hospitals on both sides, and the sick not become prisoners of war, but their persons and attendants might be priviledged and safe, as was the case betwixt the French and English in the wars of Europe.

Yet all the consequences of the sick suffering for want of necessaries——sad spectacles of human woe, presenting themselves in towns, villages and on the roads, and straggling through the country, thereby exciting the terror as well as the compassion of the inhabitants; have been ascribed to my department and the officers under me, at a time when we ourselves suffered, and called in vain for assistance from other departments, and so far as we were able, became fatigue-men and laborers to the sick and wounded, as we could procure none from the army, and, as I mentioned before, many of our attendants and nurses fled.

At the time of my greatest difficulty to procure an assortment of medicines, I gave orders to the Apothecary at Newark to assort what he had there, which was all that could be got to dispense; to issue to all applyers

for

for regimental sick, what could be spared at any rate from the hospital practice, and referred such as called upon me for medicines, to him.(x) That did not satisfy all, many expecting, as it seems, wherever they happened to be stationed, or wherever any part of the hospital was open for the reception of the sick and wounded, that they had a right to draw any medicines they wanted, and to be furnished from thence with whatever they called for, though that part was only provided for its own consumption, and the Surgeons of the hospital were willing to take care of the sick sent to them for that purpose.

In the midst of this scene of perplexity and confusion I received a note from Col. Grayson, Aid-De-Camp to your Excellency, desiring to know from you, whether I could, or whether I thought it in the line of my duty to supply the regimental Surgeons with what they wanted; to which I returned for answer, *" that I never had conceived it to be properly in the line of my duty,* though I had done every thing in my power to perform that service, for want of a better establishment, the present being in that respect contrary to every known practice, as I had always declared, and if it was ever so much expected from me I had not the means." It was then by your order that I drew up the proposed regulations for a better establishment, which I forwarded to Congress so soon as it was returned to me, and herewith send your Excellency a copy. (y) It was to no purpose that I made the same declaration to Officers and Surgeons in general, as I had done to your Excellency. Their importunities continued as great as ever.

Immediately after this, I received a charge to establish farther hospitals, to be situated more conveniently for the station of your army at that time. I recommended Hackensack. Every General officer to whom it was mentioned, approved of it, as the most suitable place of all others for the sick of the army on York-Island, there being no such convenient place on the island itself, and
the

the enemy had just made a descent above Kingsbridge. I was ordered over the river to view Hackensack, and to report what numbers of sick could be provided for at that place. On my return, I did accordingly report that if a sufficient number of carpenters and masons were set to work immediately to fit up the church, court-house, manufactory and a store house or two, &c. six or seven hundred men, and perhaps more might be accommodated in the town and neighbourhood; but it would require many workmen, and some time to prepare places for their convenient reception. I was then ordered back to carry the plan into execution with all possible diligence. I went accordingly, and next day no less than 300 men were brought into the neighbourhood for me to look after, though I was quite alone in respect to help. They daily increased in numbers, so that within a few days they amounted to upwards of a thousand. I had left instructions for Dr. *Warren*, and a number of Mates and other hospital officers to follow and attend the sick. (z)

At first we had neither bread, flour, nor fresh provisions in readiness, nor were Commissaries at hand, from whom I could obtain any help. General *Green*, to whom I sent to fort Lee for assistance, was gone over to York-island. So soon as my hands were strengthened with Dr. *Warren's* and Mr. *Zabrisky's* help, and the appointment of a Commissary and Quarter-Master, difficulties abated by degrees every day, and our affairs got into a more promising train. In the mean while the two armies having marched towards the White Plains, a battle was expected. I therefore hastened to join your Excellency. On my arrival I found the Surgeons of the General hospital, in consequence of orders from head-quarters, to look out for a place for the wounded at a convenient distance, had pitched upon the church at North-castle, as the most suitable they could meet with. I went to view it and to prepare matters if the enemy's troops should come to action.

While

Whilst we were getting in readiness, a firing of cannon was heard anew, for there had been a firing heard, the day before, at fort Washington. On learning it was at the White Plains, every Surgeon of the hospital then present set out with me, immediately, for the Plains, several Mates following, with a waggon, to bring the instruments and dressings. We fixed near the lines, and I never stirred from thence till the enemy retreated, which was about a week after; nor till your Excellency crossed the river, to hasten to the support of fort Washington. In the mean time, the situation of affairs would not permit your Excellency to give me leave to return to North Castle, but for a few hours, to give directions, and to assist in providing for the sick and wounded; an hospital Surgeon, and some times two or more, with three or four Mates, attending the whole time, at the Plains, in expectation of a second action

Here I cannot but feel for the Hospital Surgeons, who before they could obtain any quarters, except such as a few hours industry enabled them to do, in a country which was not well calculated to afford any good, were suddenly overwhelmed with numbers of sick sent to them, as well as the wounded, in time of an engagement, and whilst many of the regimental Surgeons were absent in the country, having left their corps in the field, without assistance, contrary to orders of July 3d, at a time when an engagement was considered as inevitable, there were few at hand to give any aid. Hence, whilst the hospital Surgeons were preparing matters at their proper stations in the hospital, clamors were excited against them for not being with the troops, and when they were detained at the lines, to supply the places of regimental Surgeons, who ought to have been there; the wounded, who were conveyed to to the hospital, naturally demanded the attention of the whole body of Surgeons, to administer aid to them. (&)

When I was at liberty to repair to North-Castle, all my applications for workmen, to put the hospital in order,

der, to construct chimneys, and secure the sick and wounded from cold. the effects of which were severely felt at that time, and of which it is thought some died, proved abortive. Such then as could not be accomodated here und care of Doctors Adams and McKnight, were sent to Stamford and Norwalk, to the amount of above a thousand, under the care of Doctors *Turner* and *Eustis*, Surgeons of the General hospital, and every accommodation possible was provided for them.

Before I go on with this narrative of General Hospital proceedings, I shall just observe, that in part of a day and night's time, several hundred sick and wounded, were transported from Long-Island to New-York, amidst a heavy rain, which fell during our retreat. They were landed at different wharves, and carried into different houses, whilst myself and those about me used all our endeavours to collect them together, into barracks, and hospitals I had provided for them; and although all possible care was taken to prevent it, yet may of them unavoidably suffered, though we were up great part of the night in this service.

So soon as I was able to attend that duty in person, I gave my assistance in dressing the patients, so that there was not a single one, of those wounded in the action on Long-Island, who were brought to the General hospital at New-York, that I did not dress myself; and I assisted in all operations that I knew of, wherever I was present and could attend; for I always visited as many sick officers and others, out of the hospital, by myself, and in consultation, as was any ways possible for me to do, consistent with my other calls of duty. (*aa*)

How much pains I took by writing and conversation to assist in getting the regimental Surgeons on some footing, satisfactory to them, and useful to the army, I could adduce many proofs, if required; that I never could effect it, is what I have to lament. The causes I shall not take up your time to investigate. If the plan, now before your Excellency, should take pleace either in whole,

whole, or part, it may perhaps effect that defirable purpofe, where my endeavors muft reft. (*bb*)

The orders and inftructions I have given to the Surgeons of the General hofpital, at different times, are
numerous; fome of them your Excellency read,
approved, and fubfcribed yourfelf.

Sometimes when houfes for hofpitals have been affigned me by public authority, I have met with great op-
pofition in getting poffeffion of them, from protections
in favor of the proprietors and occupiers, or others, as
in the cafe of Stuyvefants, and in thofe in the Bowry, where
a brigade of militia difpoffeffed the fick of the houfes,
affigned for that purpofe, by the New-York committee. (*cc*)

To bring this narrative of my conduct to a conclufion.
So foon as I heard of the lofs of Fort Wafhington, Fort
Lee, Hackenfack and Newark, judging your Excellency
would require my prefence, I left the beft directions
I could, for the Surgeons of the General Hofpital on
the eaft fide of Hudfon's-River, and haftened to join
you, which I did, the day after you croffed the Delaware.
I was diftreffed to find your Excellency entirely
deftitute of Surgeons, at hand, to take charge of the
wounded, in cafe of battle.

With your Excellency's approbation I proceeded to
Philadelphia, to lay this matter before Congrefs, and get
an explanation of the meaning of their refolves of
October 9th, refpecting my being ftationed on the eaft
fide of Hudfon's-river. I applied to feveral members,
and requefted an audience, but, on account of the fituation of affairs at that time, it was impoffible to obtain it.
The Congrefs was fully employed, and adjoured within
a day or two afterwards, to Maryland. The fick were
brought daily to the city, in great numbers, objects of
pity. For the care of them, I gave the beft advice I could,
to Dr. Potts, who was employed by the Council of Safety for that purpofe. Several waggon loads of medicines
and hofpital articles, which had been preferved from falling into the enemy's hands, and fent from New-York to
Newark,

Newark, and from thence to Philadelphia, were brought to the college, in no good condition. It was my care to collect from them, what was of most value, and chiefly wanted for hospital use, and send to Bethlehem. The rest, by order of Congress, were shipped to Wilmington and Christeen, where I sent a Surgeon to review, and see them repacked, in good order, and to make out an invoice of the same, and send it to Congress.

I returned to head-quarters, and that day received a letter from an honorable member, which I shewed to your Excellency, giving it as his judgement, that it was the design of Congress, I should attend to the care of the sick on the east side of Hudson's-river, and be restricted to that place: which I could not but consider as a singular restriction for a Director-General.

In obedience, however, to this resolve of Congress, I determined to repair to that station, but found it necessary to take Bethlehem in my way, as my papers and baggage, and most of the hospital Surgeons and Mates of my department were at that place, and to deliver over to some proper persons, for the use of your Excellency's army, the chief articles of the medicines I had sent there. Of these however, I reserved a few and comparatively but a few, of such as were wanted, with some few stores, likewise wanted, for the sick on this side, together with my instruments and bandages. But your Excellency having seen fit to send for these, by express, they were accordingly dispatched by the same messenger.

Of ten thousand Bandages I had prepared for use in the beginning of the campaign, what with the consumption loss, supplies to the General Hospital and regimental Surgeons, few are left.

The difficulties of attending to the wants and demands of so many sick, spread through so great a tract of country, and the clamors which have been raised, in consequence thereof, have induced me to trouble your Excellency with this long and particular detail of facts, and to request your Excellency's order for a court of Inquiry,

how

how the sick have been taken care of, in the General Hospital; composed of officers best acquainted with the rules and discipline of war, and of hospital matters; by which it may be known in what manner, agreeable to the establishment of our General Hospital, by authority of Congress, and the instructions I have received, from time to time, from Congress and your Excellency, and the information and assistance I have repeatedly applied for, provision has been made for the sick; that the nature of military hospitals, in general; and of ours in particular, may be ascertained; and if the sick have suffered more than was inevitable, from the nature, peculiar hardships and difficulties of last Campaign, the causes may be known, and a seasonable remedy applied, and those on whom any imputations have fallen, either of neglect or mismanagement, may have an opportuniy of vindicating their proceedings, before a proper tribunal, which is what I intreat for myself, and for the department under me.

I have requested Dr. *M'Knight* to take charge of these dispatches, and hope for your Excellency's answer, when leisure will permit; being with the greatest deference,

> Your Excellency's
>
> most obedient
>
> and very humble servant.
>
> JOHN MORGAN.

Fish-Kills,
February 1st. 1777.

FISH-KILLS, *February* 2, 1777.

To His Excellency General WASHINGTON.

SENSIBLE of the great difficulties, which have attended the department of Director General, owing to a great variety of causes that were not in my power to govern, by which the sick of the army suffered very much last campaign; I had just finished the memorial, which accompanies this, containing a narrative of my conduct in that department, with the hope and expectation of obtaining, from your Excellency's known humanity, and love of justice, a court of inquiry respecting it; that those causes might be examined into, and rightly understood, and I might have an opportunity of vindicating myself, before a just and candid tribunal, from any allegations that might be laid at my door, of neglect, or misconduct in the discharge of the duty of my station, according to the best of my judgement, knowledge and abilities, when Dr. Foster called to shew me your Excellency's order to him, of January 22d. It informed him, that as I was dismissed from the Director-Generalship by Congress, he was called upon as eldest Surgeon, to take charge of the hospitals on the east side of the river, till a further nomination to that post. This dismission has taken place, without my being ever notified by Congress with the reasons for it, or having been called upon, to answer for my conduct, though I had heard from a member, that heavy charges had been brought against me, for the sufferings of the sick; on which I desired him to inform Congress, that I was ready to stand the test of an examination, and requested an audience, immediately, which I could not be favoured with. This I did verbally, and afterwards applied to Congress, through him, by letter, to which I never received any answer.

On this account I drew up the present memorial, flattering myself I should obtain the wished for inquiry, from your Excellency.

A

A dismission by Congress from my station, without their having acquainted me with the nature of my supposed offences, and allowed me a previous hearing, appears to me a very severe, if not unusual proceeding. I am obliged, therefore, still to trouble your Excellency, to request your perusal of the memorial, and to express my desire that it may be laid before Congress, for their consideration —It is not, Sir, that I dispute the authority of that august Body, to appoint at pleasure, as well as to revoke their appointment of persons, to offices of rank and trust; but when a revocation is made in such a manner, as not to leave the person removed an opportunity of justifying his proceedings, in case any accusations are brought against him, it cannot fail of operating to his disadvantage, in the eyes of the world.

It is natural, therefore, to expect, and what every man has a right to hope for, that he may, though late, be heard with candor and impartiality, and to wish that a true state of his conduct, in any public department, may be known, that according to the evidence of facts it presents, he may be condemned or acquitted.

I propose to go from hence to Stamford and Norwalk, to deliver up the hospital stores, with which I have been entrusted, to Dr Foster's charge, and then proceed, as I have opportunity, to Philadelphia or Baltimore, for the settlement of my accounts.

As I shall stand in need of assistance for transporting my books, papers and baggage, I flatter myself your Excellency will be pleased to give such orders as may enable me to get them removed, without which I may suffer great delays and inconvenience.*—Wishing you success and happiness, equal to your exalted merit, I have the honour to subscribe myself, with all possible veneration,

   Your Excellency's
    most obedient
    and very humble servant.
     JOHN MORGAN.

His Excellency General Washington.

* For want of the assistance, I asked for all those articles, which were carried with the hospital stores to Danbury were entirely consumed by fire, in the late destruction of that place, April the 25th, by the incursion of the troops under Governor Tryon. The most costly of my houshold furniture, Italian history paintings done by the best masters, a choice collection of French engravings, a choice Library (exclusive of my own manuscripts, the labour of ten years) a number of rarities and specimens of natural history, to the amount of more than a thousand pounds sterling, in value, were also destroyed at Bordentown, or carried off by the enemy, at Christmas, a few weeks before this my so shameful dismission, yet whilst I was actually engaged in the service of my country. I had removed them to that place, for security, when I was first invited by Congress into the army. For such losses and services as I have sustained, in my country's cause; whilst others, of inferior rank, who have made no such sacrifices, nor sustained any losses, for lesser services, meet with promotions, and distinguished rewards ; my only returns from a grateful country. are disgrace and insults. But I sit down quiet, under this consolatory reflection, that if it be the Will of Heaven, all these things shall, in due time, work together for good.

APPENDIX.

APPENDIX.

COPY of the RESOLVES of CONGRESS, relating to the General-Hospital, and the Duties of the Director-General, Directors of Hospitals, Surgeons of Hospitals and Regiments, and to the Provision for the Sick, &c.

In CONGRESS, Thursday, July 17, 1775.

RESOLVED, That for the establishment of an Hospital for an ARMY, consisting of 20,000 men, the following officers and other attendants be appointed, with the following allowance and pay.

A Director-General and Chief Physician, his pay 4 Dollars per day.
4 Surgeons, per day, each - one and a third, do.
1 Apothecary, - one and a third, do.
20 Mates, each per day, - two-thirds, do.
1 Clerk, - - - two-thirds, do.
2 Storekeepers, each - 4 Dollars per Month.
1 Nurse to every 10 sick, one-fifteenth of a Dollar per day, or 2 Dollars per Month.
Labourers occasionally.

THE DUTY OF THE ABOVE OFFICERS, viz.

Director and Chief Physician to furnish medicines, bedding and all other necessaries; to pay for the same; superintend the whole; and to make his report to, and receive orders from the Commander in Chief.

Surgeons,

Surgeons, Apothecaries and Mates, to visit and attend the sick, and the Mates to obey the orders of the Physician, Surgeons and Apothecary.

Matron, to superintend the Nurses, bedding, &c.

Nurses to attend the sick, and obey the Matrons orders.

Clerk, to belong to the Director and Storekeeper.

Storekeeper, to receive and deliver the bedding, and other necessaries, by order of the Director.

Extract from the Minutes.

CHARLES THOMSON, Secretary.

RESOLVED, That the appointment of the four Surgeons, and the Apothecary, be left to the Director General and Chief Physician.—That the Mates be appointed by the Surgeons; and that the number do not exceed twenty; and that the number be not kept in constant pay, unless the sick and wounded should be so numerous as to require the attendance of twenty, and to be dismissed as circumstances will admit; for which purpose, the pay is fixed by the day, that they may only receive pay for actual service.

That the Clerk, Storekeepers and Nurses, be appointed by the Director.

Extract from the Minutes.

CHARLES THOMSON, Secretary.

By Order of CONGRESS.

JOHN HANCOCK, President.

In CONGRESS, September 14, 1775.

RESOLVED, That SAMUEL STRINGER, Esq; be appointed Director of the Hospital, and Chief Physician and Surgeon, for the ARMY in the Northern Department.

That the pay of the said SAMUEL STRINGER, Esq; as Director, Physician and Surgeon, be four Dollars per day.

That he be authorized, and have power to appoint a number of Surgeons-Mates under him, not exceeding four.

That the pay of said Mates, be two-thirds of a Dollar per day.

That the number be not kept in constant pay, unless the sick and wounded be so numerous as to require the constant attendance of four, and be diminished as circumstances shall admit, for which reason the pay is fixed by the day, that they may only receive pay for actual service.

That the Deputy Commissary General be directed to pay Doctor STRINGER, for the medicines he has purchased for the use of the ARMY, and that he purchase and forward such other medicines as General SCHUYLER, shall, by his warrant direct for the use of the said ARMY.

A Copy from the Minutes.

CHARLES THOMSON, Secretary.

By Order of the CONGRESS.

JOHN HANCOCK, President.

IN CONGRESS, July 17, 1776.

RESOLVED, That the number of the Hospital Surgeons and Mates, be increased in proportion to the augmentation of the ARMY, not exceeding one Surgeon and five Mates, to every five thousand men; to be reduced, when the ARMY is reduced, or when there is no further occasion for so great a number.

That as many persons be employed in the several Hospitals, in quality of Storekeepers, Stewards, Managers and Nurses, as are necessary for the good of the service for the time being, to be appointed by the Directors of the several Hospitals.

That the several regimental chests of medicines, and chirurgical instruments which now are, or hereafter shall be in the possession of the regimental Surgeons, be subject to the inspection and inquiry of the respective Directors of Hospitals and the Director General, and that the said regimental Surgeons shall from time to time, when thereto required, render account of the said medicines and instruments to the said Directors; or if there be no Director in any particular department, to the Director General; the said account to be transmitted to the Director General, and by him to the Congress; and the medicines and instruments not used by any regimental Surgeon, to be returned when the regiment is reduced, to the respective Directors, and an account thereof by them rendered to the Director General, and by him to this Congress.

That the several Directors of Hospitals in the several departments, and the regimental Surgeons where there is no Director, shall transmit to the Director General, regular returns of the number of Surgeons-Mates, and other officers employed under them, their names and pay; also an account of the expences and furniture of the Hospital under their direction; and that the Director General make report of the same, from time to time, to the Commander in Chief, and to this Congress.

That

That the several Regimental and Hospital Surgeons, in the several departments, make weekly returns of their sick to their respective Directors, in the said department.

That no regimental Surgeon be allowed to draw upon the Hospital of his department, for any stores except medicines and instruments, and that when any sick person shall require other stores, they shall be received into the said Hospital, and the rations of the said sick persons be stopped, so long as they are in said Hospital; and that the Directors of the several Hospitals report to the Commissary, the names of the sick when received into, and when discharged from the Hospital, and make a like return to the Board of Treasury.

That all extra expences, for bandages, old linen, and other articles necessary for the service, incurred by any regimental Surgeon, be paid by the Director of that department, with the approbation of the Commander thereof.

That no more medicines belonging to the Continent, be disposed of till further orders of Congress:—That the pay of the Hospital Surgeons, be increased to one Dollar and two-thirds of a Dollar by day; the pay of the Hospital Mates be increased to one Dollar by the day; and the pay of the Hospital Apothecary be increased to one Dollar and two-thirds of a Dollar per day; and that the Hospital Surgeons and Mates take rank of regimental Surgeons and Mates.

That the Director General and the several Directors of Hospitals, be impowered to purchase, with the approbation of the respective departments, medicines and instruments for the use of their respective Hospitals, and draw upon the Paymaster for the same, and make report of such purchase to Congress.

JOHN HANCOCK, President.

A true Copy from the Resolves of Congress.
J. REED, Adjutant-General.

IN CONGRESS, July 20, 1776.

RESOLVED, That Doctor SENTERS, be recommended to Doctor MORGAN, who is desired to examine him, and if he find him qualified, to employ him in the Hospital as Surgeon.

Extract from the Minutes.

CHARLES THOMSON, Secretary.

DOCTOR STRINGER, having presented a petition to Congress, the substance of which was,— " quest an explanation of the resolves of Congress, re the nature and extent of his own, as well as D ORGAN's appointment."

 NGRESS, August 20, 1776.

 mmittee appointed to consider of Doctor s petition, report as follows :
 . MORGAN was appointed Director and Physician in Chief of the American Hos-

at Doctor STRINGER, was appointed Di- and Physician of the Hospital, in the Northern   ent, only.

IN CONGRESS, October 9, 1776.

RESOLVED, That no regimental Hospitals be in future allowed, in the neighbourhood of the General Hospital. That

That JOHN MORGAN, Esq; provide and superintend a Hospital, at a proper distance from the camp, for the ARMY posted on the East side of Hudson's River.

That WILLIAM SHIPPEN, Esq; provide and superintend a Hospital for the ARMY in the State of New-Jersey.

That each of the Hospitals be supplied "by the respective Directors," with such a number of Surgeons, Apothecaries, Surgeons-Mates and other Assistants; and also with such quantities of medicines and bedding, and other necessaries, as they shall judge expedient.

That they make weekly returns to Congress, and the Commander in Chief, of the officers and assistants of each denomination; and also the number of sick and deceased, in their respective Hospitals.

That the regimental Surgeons be directed to send to the General Hospital such officers and soldiers of their respective regiments, as confined by wounds, or other disorders, shall require Nurses or constant attendance, and from time to time apply to the Quarter-Master General, or his Deputy, for convenient waggons for this purpose: Also, that they apply to the Directors in their respective departments for medicines and other necessaries.

That the wages of Nurses be augmented to one Dollar a week.

That the Commanding Officer of each regiment, be directed once a week to send a commission officer, to visit the sick of his respective regiment, in the General Hospital, and report their state to them.

Extract from the Minutes.

CHARLES THOMSON, Secretary.

To His Excellency
GENERAL WASHINGTON,
Commander in Chief, &c.

General-Hospital, at Cambridge, February, 1776.

SIR,

THE nature of my station having led me to make many reflexions, on the situation of the sick, in the army, and the means required for their relief, I have been anxious to lay before your Excellency, what appears to me, to be necessary for this purpose, and wanting to render the business of the General Hospital more easy and compleat. I am desirous to suggest to you, what benefits may be supposed to arise, from the establishment of regimental Surgeons and Mates; what are, and ought to be looked upon, as the duties of their place; to shew the insufficiency of any powers hitherto given them, " by Congress or your Excellency," to supply the defects " of their station, which they at present labour under," without some fixed regulations, and without some provision being made for them, that, for ought I see, they are almost wholly destitute of, and which they are at a loss how to remedy, and without which they can be of little service to the sick. This I am willing to undertake at large, and to point out some plan, for putting it in their power to supply the sick, of their regiments, whilst allowed to remain under their care, " with whatever is supposed requsite for the purpose." At the same time, I am desirous of pointing out a method of regulating the expences of the General hospital, and of furnishing the sick in it with many necessaries and refreshments, " which they at present want," in the most suitable and least chargeable ways. To do it properly would be a work of time, and I find little leisure at present for a task that would require

some

some vacancy from the daily avocations of my business, to effect. Yet I keep the design in view, when other necessary calls of duty will permit.

"But although I cannot perform this work fully now, yet it is necessary to say something; our circumstances and situation require a general explanation of what is wanting." The nature and design of a General hospital is so little understood, and my particular duty so much mistaken, both by regimental Surgeons and other officers; so many expectations are formed, and so many things looked for, from me, which are impossible to be complied with, that I apprehend it to be absolutely necessary that certain regulations be fixed upon, for the better government of the hospital, myself, and the Surgeons and officers of the hospital under me, as well as of the regimental Surgeons, which all ought to know; by which they may be respectively kept within their line of duty, without interference with each other, and which every officer who has any thing to do with the sick may be apprized of, to prevent mistakes.

To begin with my own department, I beg leave to refer your Excellency to the particular duty which is assigned by the Congress to the Director-General, and chief Physician of the hospital, and to the powers with which he is vested.

His DUTY is to furnish medicines, bedding, and all other necessaries; to pay for the same, to superintend the whole, TO MAKE HIS REPORT TO and RECEIVE HIS ORDERS FROM THE COMMANDER IN CHIEF, &c.

Your Excellency will be pleased to observe that I have never had "any mention made to me of," nor received the least instructions concerning either regimental Surgeons or regimental sick; and yet there is not perhaps a single regimental Surgeon, and even but few officers who do not suppose they have a right to insist upon my furnishing every regiment, as well the established soldiery, as the militia, with whatever articles they are pleased to demand from the hospital, as though it was a store house,

E

house, or magazine for the whole army, "and not confined, in the intention of its establishment, to the purpose of taking care of those sick and wounded, that might be reported to it as proper objects, and admitted accordingly." Thus, besides what medicines are allowed, as well to the militia as to every other regiment in the army, regimental Surgeons have a custom of making demands on the General hospital for instruments of surgery, bandages, linnen, tourniquets, wine, rum, sugar, molasses, chocolate, coffee, butter, candles, soap, brandy, raisins, rice, flour, Indian meal and fresh meat. They suppose I am obliged to comply with any order signed by a "regimental" Surgeon or Mate, for those articles, in any quantity they see fit to demand. I have been informed, that some officers have taken it much amiss, if they wanted veal or mutton, that they could not have it from the hospital, "on sending for it for their own tables." What is more unaccountable, no regimental Surgeons ever thought it their duty to make any report to me of the state of their sick, to leave me room to judge of the propriety of issuing, or of refusing to issue out whatever stores they were pleased to call for.

To shew in what light the hospital is viewed, and my duty as Director of it, accounts of soldiers that I know nothing of, and who have never been reported to me for directions about them, are sent to me for payment, and from all quarters, near and afar off. Officers who are sick in the country, at a distance from the army, under country practitioners, send in their accounts by those Doctors for me to discharge.* So numerous and unreasonable are the demands of officers, regimental Surgeons, "and others, directed by them to the Director-General of the hospital for payment," that were all those demands gratified, the expences of the sick, as the Commissary-General hath often remarked, would exceed all the expences of the whole army besides.

"To give a pretext for the propriety of their claims, they

---

* See W. M. Phil'ps's account, subjoined to this letter.

they plead their inability of being furnished elsewhere with what they want;" the cry of the regimental Surgeons is, there is no provision made for us. "My anfwer is, nor have I any orders to provide for any but what are under my own direction in the General hofpital. They afk where they are to get inftruments and dreffings, and what they want for the fick under their care, or of what ufe are they, if left unprovided. I refer them to their commanding officers, and to make reprefentations of their fituation to them, to apply to Congrefs to eftablifh means of furnifhing what they want; whatever orders are given me, they fhall be obeyed, but I cannot go beyond my inftructions." Do they imagine that 4 Surgeons and 20 Mates (which are all the Surgeons allowed me in the General hofpital, for an army of 20,000 men) employed in attending all the fick and wounded that are fent to them from the whole army, and as they can find, or make liefure from that employ, conftantly bufied in preparing lint, bandages, compreffes, fplints, tourniquets and other dreffings for hofpitals ufe in cafe of any confiderable action, muft be fubjected to their demands, and obliged to unfurnifh the hofpital, and give up the labour of their hands, to three or four fcore of regimental Surgeons and Mates, who were to have no trouble themfelves, in making any preparations for their own ufe.

Has not your Excellency "recommended the ftricteft oeconomy, and" informed me that from the eftimates given in to Congrefs, it was computed that £.10,000 per ann. was fufficient to anfwer all the demands of the General hofpital, "and that you were apprehenfive the expences already exceeded what was imagined a fufficiency?" The falaries of all the officers in employ, the nurfes and attendants nearly equal to half that fum, without taking into the account the expence of hofpital furniture, bedding, blankets, medicines and inftruments. From fuch limited funds, for the fupport of the General hofpital, can it be expected that between thirty and forty regiments fhall

draw

draw supplies intended only for the General hospital itself?

In this situation, I humbly request your Excellency's instructions. "Be pleased to consider that" my COMMISSION only extends to the care of the HOSPITAL itself; and yet every regimental Surgeon, apparently, expects me to supply him with whatever he wants, and to prepare every thing to his hand, or to lay the odium of his deficiency at my door.

This application of mine does not proceed from any desire or inclination to shrink from any service I can render them; but, if this service (contrary to my present duty) is required of me, the means must be established, and I must receive positive instructions for it, lest I be deemed guilty of neglecting, or not sufficiently providing for my own department, for the sake of those who are not comprehended within it.

On the whole, I think it my duty to represent to your Excellency, that I have thought it incumbent on me, to give directions to the stores-keepers of the General hospital to issue no stores from thence, on the bare order of any regimental Surgeon, except Indian meal, rice or oatmeal, and if they want wine, rum, sugar, or other the like stores, they must produce an order for these, countersigned by me, and take a receipt for the same to make them accountable for the disposal of what they thus receive, if called upon I have directed the apothecary to issue out medicines to them, for the use of each regiment, in such quantities, as their present occasions may require, but so as not to unfurnish the hospital, or exhaust the stock, faster than I can get a fresh supply. To enable, you, Sir, to form some judgment of what is necessary for the purpose, I must observe that such an army as is now on foot, will require an additional sum of two thousand pounds sterling per annum at least for the use of the regimental Surgeons, over and above what is necessary for the supply of the General hospital itself. And it will be for ever needy, and even destitute of capital

tal medicines, if not speedily furnished with a fresh supply, to the amount of two or three thousand pounds medicines being very scarce and dear.

Another observation I beg leave to make is, that every regiment ought to have a small portable chest, for the whole year at once, and be provided with instruments, bandages and dressings.

It is not with any view to reflect upon the regimental Surgeons, but for the better purpose of procuring them relief from their difficulties, that I am obliged to inform your Excellency, that there are but very few of them, as far as I can learn, who have what can be called even a tolerable supply of any, even the most essential articles for regimental Surgeons, instruments or bandages, and that they are deluding themselves with a false opinion, that in case of action, every regimental Surgeon will be immediately furnished with those articles from the hospital I fear, from this circumstances, most of them would be extremely at a loss what to do, or be even useless in a battle.

I would therefore recommend to your Excellency, that " a person be appointed for the purpose," and instructions given for furnishing a regimental chest of medicines, with instruments, lint, tow and bandages, &c. for each regiment ; that orders be issued, that every regimental Surgeon make out a report of what he has of those articles in readiness, and a representation of what he may further want, to be collected together, in order to judge of their present deficiencies ; and that the regimental chests be inspected from time to time As continual complaints are made of the ignorance and unfitness of many called regimental Surgeons and Mates for that post, and I find them generally unacquainted with what duties are to be expected of them, in that station ; I would advise, " if it be thought practicable under present circumstances," that some kind of examination be made of their respective abilities, by a chosen committee; being a practice observed in all countries, which is essential

tial to the service, and is now established in the middle colonies.

"I have been amazed to hear it said, and that it should have been thought, even by some members of Congress, that little use was expected from regimental Surgeons, where there was a General hospital; and this has been given to me as a reason for their being so much neglected, or so ill provided with the means of being useful, and is, perhaps, the best reason that can be given that there are comparatively so few amongst them, at present, of any tolerable education, experience or knowledge in the business and duties of the station." Before I put an end to this letter, I must beg your indulgence whilst I trouble your Excellency with two observations more. The first is, that regimental hospitals and regimental Surgeons, under proper regulations and subordination to the General hospital, are absolutely necessary, and, in my opinion, may be made extremely serviceable in an army; secondly, were matters so well regulated that whenever any soldier was taken ill, whether sent to the General hospital, or whether he continued with his regiment, under the care of his proper Surgeon; if his rations were stopped for the time, and paid for in money, it would, in my opinion, be sufficient or nearly so, provided he was dieted as he ought to be for a sick man, and as he is directed to be, in the General hospital, not only to pay for his diet, but to supply him with every necessary refreshment without any, "or with little" additional expence to the publick, from the stores of the General hospital. To prove this, may require an explanation, which I shall willingly give when called for.* Permit

* General Parsons, I am informed by the Commissary-General, has, to his great credit, since tried the experiment, and on this plan the sick of his brigade were provided last summer with every thing necessary and comfortable to men in their situation, and there was a saving of sixty pounds lawful, after every article was paid for, from the stoppage of the sick men's rations, and receiving the amount in cash, in lieu of rations.

Permit me, Sir, to conclude with this remark that if the sick in regiments are to be supplied at a public expence, that expence ought to be a regimental charge, and may well enough be included in the abstract of the regiment. The General hospital having nothing to do with regimental sick, till they are reported to, and admitted as proper objects, ought not to be burdened with the expence. In this manner, the expence of "maintaining the sick in regimental hospitals will be known," and that of supporting a General hospital, unmixed with the former, may be pretty exactly ascertained from experience; nor would it be charged with enormous accounts, which the General hospital, properly speaking, has nothing to do with.

I remain,

Your Excellency's

most obedient

humble servant,

JOHN MORGAN.

(*b*) P. S. I would observe to your Excellency, that the sum allowed by Congress for the payment of the store-keepers is so insignificant as four dollars a month; about half the wages of a common soldier; though it is a place of great trust, and requires talents and application to business, as well as integrity to perform it well.

The pay of nurses is fixt by Congress at half a dollar per week. Whilst it is so low, we shall never be able to furnish good nurses, or in short any nurses, in proportion to the number wanted for the sick. They complain of
their

their pay, and are jealous that more is allowed, but that part of it is stopped: Most of them say they were promised a dollar per week. I have only paid them what is allowed by my instructions.

There is a necessity for having occasional officers in the General hospital, of whom no mention is made in the establishment by Congress. Some such I have found here on my arrival. They remain without pay, nor is their pay settled. I have neither confirmed their appointment, nor have I dismissed them, instructions being wanted.

It is necessary that I report to your Excellency the dismission of five Mates from the General hospital, as, by order of Congress, they were only employed by the day; and they have refused to submit to any examination of their qualifications.

N. B. ☞ *The above Letter is printed from the original rough draft of it, wrote in haste, and delivered to General Washington, and which he returned for a fair copy, in which the lines and words, comprehended betwixt inverted comma's, are interlineations, perhaps a few of them additions, but none others are. I think proper to mention this as I would not willingly incur the charge of altering the sense of the original, or making an addition, but of a few words, to render the sense more obvious, or compleat, for the ease of the reader.*

☞ *It is proper to remark here, that this very letter was read two several days before the medical committee of Congress, in the conference I had with them in June last, when I went to Philadelphia for that purpose, and I then laid before them, for their consideration, the several regulations, which did not appear in their resolves till near a month after.*

Amongst

Amongst other accounts I had before me, at the time of writing this letter, I shall select one, as it is undersigned by persons in a public station, who are well known, and I doubt not, if necessary, will attest the truth of the copy, of which I still have all the original accounts in my possession.

WILLIAM MESERVE PHILIPS, being a soldier in Col. John Glover's regiment, to the Selectmen of the town of Marblehead, Dr.

To sundries supplied him by sundry persons while sick with the small-pox, viz. £. s d. q.

			£	s	d	q
1775, Aug. Capt. James Mugford's Bill for Amount,			1	12	4	
Benjamin Needham's Bill	do.			13	8	
Elizabeth Smith's Bill	do.		2	8		
Richard Tarr's Bill	do.		5	3	4	
Thomas Hartshorn's Bill	do.			8	11	
William Wait's Bill	do.		1	1	0	1
N. Dement's Bill	do.		3	16	0	
Jeremiah Procter's Bill	do.			8	9	2
Cornelius Philips's,	do.		1	13	1	1
		£.	17	4	6	

Marblehead, 11th of December, 1775.

Errors excepted.

James Mugford,	Edward Fettyplace,	} Selectmen.
St. Philips,	Jeremiah Procter,	
Wm. Doliber,	Robert Hooper, tert.	

Marblehead, Dec. 14, 1775.

Sir,

Please to pay Deacon Wm. Doliber or order, seventeen pounds four shillings and six pence, it being the amount of the charges of Wm. Meserve Phillips's, having the small-pox in this town, as per account above, and you'll oblige your humble servants,

| James Mugford, | Edward Fettyplace, | } Selectmen. |
| St. Phillips, | William Doliber, | |

To John Morgan, Director-General.

To gratify the curiosity of such who may wish to know some of the principal articles of those charges, I have selected them from the several accounts, and classed them as follows.

	£.	s.	d.
To N. Damen for 19 Day's Attendance in Nursing, at 2-thirds of a Dollar per Day,	3	16	0
To Elizabeth Smith's Account of ditto,	2	8	0
To Richard Tarr's for do. at Pest-House, i. e. S. P. Hosp.	5	3	4
	£. 11	7	4
To Beef, Lamb, Mutton and Salt Pork, at 7d. l. m. p. lb.	1	11	10 2
To the Doctor for 4 visits, a vomit and six fever powders		8	11
The other Articles, including New-England and other Rum, (to the amount of sixteen Quarts) Wine, BRAD FOR THE MULPOCX and Syrrup of SESFEN, Candles, &c.	3	16	4 2
Total amount (equal to 57 Dollars 2-6.)	£. 17	4	6

From the Doctor's visits and accounts (which must be confessed to be very low) compared with the diet, salt pork, wine and rum, &c. it must appear how necessary such an expensive attendance was for a private soldier, in the small-pox and what idea was entertained of the duty of a Director-General, if liable to pay such accounts.

I had also before me, at this time, a copy of the drafts of one regimental Surgeon at Cambridge, upon the store of the General Hospital, for above an hundred gallons, or an hogshead of rum; wine, loaf and brown sugar, and molasses in proportion; and to shew the extreme necessity, one pint of oatmeal was added to the list, being for one regiment only; all within the space of about six weeks; and yet there was no return made of the sick, but all demanded on the faith of an order, signed by a regimental Surgeon or Mate.

I shall here likewise, remark, that, when after regimental Surgeons were repeatedly called upon, by general orders, to make reports of the state of the sick, although many of them never complied at all with those orders, amongſt thoſe who did make their returns, ſome individuals reported above an hundred, each But when Doctor Foſter, then Surgeon in the General hoſpital, attended, by my directions, to viſit, in particular, Col. Parſons's regiment, of which the Surgeon was ſuddenly taken ill, in order to receive ſuch as were proper objects, into the General hoſpital ; on calling over the liſt by name to examine their caſes, there were but few of them, who were not found, and did not acknowledge themſelves, to be fit for duty.

In ſome returns, of which I took care to keep the originals, forty waiters and upwards were included on the ſick liſt, to exempt ſo many from duty. Some regimental Surgeons made a practice of ſelling recommendations to furloughs and diſcharges ; for which only one, out of the number ſuppoſed to merit that diſtinction, was drummed out of the army, for ſuch mean and ſcandalous practices. Had all who deſerved it, met the ſame reward, it would have reduced the liſt very conſiderably. Cordials and refreſhments were drawn by others, from the ſtores of the General hoſpital, which by the parts ſome of the officers took in ſupporting the unreaſonable demands of thoſe men, gave room for many to believe they ſhared in the plunder themſelves.

Is it any wonder, on being repeatedly informed of theſe particulars, that I put a total ſtop to the unauthorized practice of the regimental Surgeons drawing ſtores from the General hoſpital, without obliging them to be accountable for the ſame ? Is it a matter of ſurprize that regimental Surgeons and officers of that caſt, ſhould manifeſt a declared enmity againſt one, who contravened their ſhameful meaſures ; or that they ſhould have influence with ſome of the privates, in concert with whom they preyed on the vitals of the publick, to declaim againſt the General hoſpital, whilſt thoſe who were proper objects for it, and had once experienced the benefit of that inſtitution, were glad to have recourſe to it, as often as they ſtood in need ?

When

When the estimate of hospital expences was so very low, and such œconomy for I may not call it parsimony, was manifested in the pay allowed to the hospital officers by former resolves of Congress, so different from the generous munificence of the present day, that four dollars per month, was then thought a sufficiency for the hospital store-keepers. [Great proof of its being the intention of Congress, that they should issue stores, to the amount of many hundred thousand dollars per annum, to regimental Surgeons;] is it any wonder that I would not suffer regimental Surgeons to draw, *ad libitum*, for whatever their unbounded appetites and fancies craved from the General hospital; or, when I discovered so many arts put in practice, to defraud the publick, that I would pay no accounts of soldiers, out of the hospital, contracted without my knowledge, and out of the sphere of my department? Had I allowed myself to be drawn into this snare, who can tell what limits they would have set to their growing demands? Some large accounts of private practitioners, were brought to me; from more than an hundred miles distance. Some of them had charged near five pounds, a day, for attendance on common soldiers, who ailed but little. Had I passed those accounts, would it not have been at the risk of my own reputation? but why mention reputation? Have I not suffered more obloquy from the malignity of such men, on account of saving prodigious sums to the Continent, with great toil, but no possible advantage to myself, than some others for engulphing the public monies? Such are the rewards of care and exactness in business to serve one's country; glorious pledges of liberty! when officers of rank are to be forced from their stations, to make way for undermining and ambitious men, on their partial representations, without any hearing! *oh fortunatos nimium, sua si bona norint agricolæ!*

(*b*) The

(*b*) The want of sufficient assistance from other departments was attended with many and great inconveniences. For example, When it was thought necessary to establish a General hospital above Kingsbridge, in the neighbourhood of that wing of the army commanded by Major-General HEATH in October, after the proper places were pitched upon for that design, I called upon the Deputy-Quarter-Master-General for workmen and materials, to put the several houses in order, to build chimnies, to construct births, and to make suitable apartments for the sick and wounded. The Q. M. General being then at Philadelphia, the D. Q. M. General informed me that every carpenter and mason under his direction in the army were engrossed, and could not be taken off from their present employ. He advised me to make application to General HEATH, for an order, to obtain as many of the militia, or other soldiers who were proper workmen, to be drafted from their respective regiments under his command, as would suffice for the present occasion. I sent to General HEATH for this purpose. The answer I received was, that the General did not chuse to meddle with any thing to be done in the Quarter-Master-Generals department. When General MIFFLIN, Quarter-Master-General, returned some time after from Philadelphia, where he was then gone, I procured an order from him on his Deputy, for a dozen carpenters and masons; but they could not be spared from other business; and not one was sent to me all the time I remained on York-Island, from the biginning of October, to the time of my going over to Hackinsack, after the middle of the month, when the army began to retreat to the White Plains.

The same thing happened frequently at other times and places particularly at North Castle; when, after earnest applications made by myself and the Surgeons of the General hospital, to that department, and orders were given by the Quarter-Master-General himself, or his Deputy, on the Commander of the Artificers, they could

not

not be procured, it being always declared that all hands were engaged by prior orders, for other purposes of the army. I do not mention these difficulties with a view to reflect upon, either the Quarter-Master-General, or his Deputy. Men of greater activity, or greater abilities for the respective posts, I do not imagine can be produced: No, were they wanting in inclination to give me all the assistance they were capable of affording. But if they had it not in their power, still the inconveniences were no less on account of that inclination; yet was I to suffer, and be blamed for wants which neither the whole army, nor perhaps the Congress itself; at least no other persons were capable of making a timely provision for, and to be answerable, as it would seem for all the misfortunes of the campaign?

When I was at Hackinsack I was expresly forbidden by the General, to draft any workmen from the army. My whole dependence was placed on such as I could meet with in the country, and which I ought to have had from the Quarter-Master-General's department; few were to be found in the neighbourhood of the army, when affairs went on otherwise than prosperously. Nor had I any company or guards allotted to me, for any purposes of the General Hospital, when I first went to Hackinsack, and men were wanting to go after provisions and for other necessaries, besides waiting on the sick and wounded, that were hourly brought in great numbers, without any persons whatever to attend them.

Once, indeed, when the sick became very numerous, about ten days before the retreat from New-York, and when I stood in greater need than usual, of an increase of labourers and waiters in the General Hospital, and there were no men to be had in the city, who were willing to engage in that service, after repeated applications for that purpose, it was given out in general orders, that fifty men should be drafted from the line, who were allotted to that duty. No day passed without making personal application myself, to the officers appointed to direct

rect the performance of this order, yet a week paſſed before it was complied with. When the men were paraded, and marched to the New-York college, to receive their orders from me, at what hoſpitals they were to be employed, and how to be diſpoſed of, they declared they would not remain there. They ſaid they were cheated, having been told they were ordered for quite a different duty. I reaſoned with them, and ſhewed the neceſſity there was of their help, promiſed to make their ſervices as eaſy and agreeable to them as poſſible, and to allow them each a gill of rum per day, if they behaved well, and threatened them, if they left me, to report them as guilty of diſobeying the General's orders. They feigned acquieſcence. Yet, by next day, moſt of them had deſerted from the hoſpital, and returned to their companies, although, beſides the ſick, there were near one hundred wounded to attend. Such was the diſcipline of the army at that time. Before I could take any ſtep to have theſe men called to account, I was ordered over to Newark, to provide accommodations for the ſick at that place, in the midſt of which, great part of the remaining Waiters, and ſome of the Nurſes left the hoſpital.

AS the following letters, ſelected from a number of others, written by me, to different members of Congreſs, on the buſineſs of my department, bear teſtimony to the pains I took to give full and timely information to that Body. of the ſtate of the ſick in the General hoſpital and the army, of the deficiencies and inconveniences both laboured under, for want of ſuitable regulations, and of what ſupplies were wanting, in time for affording more effectual relief, at leaſt in many inſtances, had that information been duly attended to by Congreſs, I need not make any apology for publiſhing them in this place, at full length, and in their original dreſs. I am not ſure, if I were to give only extracts, or an abridgment of them, that it would be ſatisfactory. If they appear rather prolix to the reader, I muſt beg leave to inform him, that it was for want of leiſure they were not more conciſe;

nor

nor did I expect at the time they were written, that I should ever think it necessary to print them. Besides, in business of so much importance, I imagine it will be considered as a less fault, to be minute and particular, and even to repeat the same things, in the hurry of writing, than to give so cursory a relation, as to fail of answering the design of affording full information of whatever falls under the writer's notice, that may inform those in office of the true state of his department, and be any further inducement to them, than they already have, to exert themselves, in giving all the timely assistance that is needful, to remedy every want, or remove every inconvenience under which it labours.

On my arrival from Cambridge, at New-York, the latter end of May, 1776, I found several orders, drawn upon me, from the Northern Army, for supplies of medicines and instruments, and particularly for a large supply of medicines from Doctor Stringer, Director in that department. I heard from a number of officers, of great rank, who were just returned from Philadelphia, that Congress expected me, as Director General, to order the necessary supplies of Hospital stores, for the Northern department. I had received no such orders. As I thought proper regulations were wanting, to ascertain the respective limits of authority, intended by Congress to be vested in myself, and the several Directors, I requested leave to go to Philadelphia, to obtain an audience of a committee of Congress, on that subject, which I obtained. I left proposals of several regulations with that committee, for introducing order into the different branches of the General Hospital department. Amongst others, I proposed that the several Directors and Superintendants of Hospitals, should be ordered and impowered to provide their respective departments with Hospital stores, without depending on me for supplies; it being impossible for me, circumstanced as I was, to answer their demands. Nothing was determined till a month afterwards. In the mean while,

while, upon my return to New-York, Doctor Potts, who had a separate charge of certain Hospitals, which were to be established to the Northward applyed to me for the appointment of Surgeons and other Hospital officers to act under him, and for a farther supply of medicines, than he had yet obtained. He expressed it as his opinion, that he was obliged, in duty, to look to me for assistance, and said he should depend upon me only, as head of the department, for every thing of which he should stand in need. At the same time, Doctor Lind, applied to me for medicines, for General Sullivan's army, on which, I wrote the following Letter.

New-York, June 25, 1775.

TO THE HONORABLE

SAMUEL ADAMS, Esq;

Member of the Medical Committee of Congress.

SIR,

THE state of the army in Canada, according to Dr. Lind's account, (who is just arrived from thence, by order of General Sullivan, for a supply of medicines,) is truly deplorable. I have seen no return of the sick, but he assures me, that in the beginning of this month, there were no less than 1800 men down with the small-pox; and the total of sick and unfit for duty, amounted to 3,300 men; and he says, they have no medicines: Such a report is scarcely credible, but you may learn the particulars, yourself, from him, as he intends going to Philadelphia.

General Gates sets out to-morrow, to take the command of the army in Canada. Dr. Potts will accompany

pany him. I have therefore given orders to supply him, from the General Hospital, with a large chest of such medicines as I can best spare; and which can be got ready to-morrow before his departure. Upon looking into Dr. Potts's commission, I find he is appointed Physician and Surgeon in the department of Canada; but whether it be of a regiment, or in the Hospital, is not specified; nor does it shew whether it is the intention of Congress, to vest him with the power of a Director, in the General Hospital: Nor can I learn, what appointment Dr. Stringer has, or what is the nature of his commission.

From all I am able to learn, every thing in the medical department, in Canada, displays one scene of confusion and anarchy: Nor have the Congress taken upon itself, to establish, or vested any person whatever, with a power sufficient to establish a General Hospital in Canada.

The Congress cannot, in my humble opinion, be too speedy in determining what steps are to be taken for this purpose, and for settling a due subordination amongst the Surgeons there. It would be of particular use, that the intentions of Congress were made known in respect to Dr. Stringer and Dr. Potts, whether either of them is to be considered as Director, by appointment of Congress, and which of them; or whether they are both to be looked upon as Surgeons depending on, and acting by instructions from me. I have never seen Dr. Stringer's commission. In either case, they will require more help than they have at present; and in the latter, I suppose I ought to have the appointment of three or four more Hospital Surgeons, an Apothecary, and a sufficiency of Mates in that department, without diminishing the number I have allowed me for the army at New-York, as I have none here that are superfluous. Other officers, as a Storekeeper, Stewart and Matron, are also wanted in Canada, with Nurses and occasional Labourers. Whatever is determined on, in respect to

these

these matters, I should be glad to know immediately. Till then, my hands are tied up, and the army suffering for want of help. I am not sure that our disgrace and misfortunes in Canada are not owing, in a great measure, to the shameful proceedings of the Surgeons, in spreading the small-pox by innoculation, amongst the soldiery, in face of the enemy. Instead of innoculating the soldiery, under like circumstances before Boston, General Washington, upon my representation, continued to keep in pay a Surgeon and Mate, to attend all that fell ill of the small-pox. A Hospital was fixed for their reception only, in a retired place, and a guard set round it, and all communication betwixt it and the army was cut off; and so soon as any one was seized with the infection, of whatever rank, he was sent to the small-pox Hospital. By this means, every inconveniency, arising from the appearance of the small-pox, was prevented, and the army effectually secured from danger, from that quarter.

Had there been a General Hospital in Canada, there would have been better orders, and some subordination observed, which is now wholly wanting; and it is to be feared, that whilst the Congress, occupied in a multiplicity of weighty concerns, can proceed but slowly on this matter, the opportunity may be lost. Rather than postpone, however, so important a concern, would it not be right to place full confidence and power in a proper person, capable to arrange these matters, as they ought to be, with ample authority for the purpose, rather than suffer a loss of men, to the discouragement of the whole army, for want of a due provision being made for the sick and wounded.

If the Congress will fix on the means and manner of establishing a General Hospital at Canada, it will ease me of much trouble; but if they are not at leisure, or not sufficiently acquainted with what is the proper manner, and will order me to do it for them, giving me such power as they think adequate, I will do the best I can;

to effect this desirable end immediately. Excuse, Sir, my dwelling so earnestly on this subject; it is of the utmost consequence to the service, and delays are dangerous. I cannot expect to receive instructions, on this matter, from General Washington; he supposes, that I understand the affairs of this department, and relies wholly on me for every thing which relates to it. *But I neither durst, nor will I presume, to meddle in affairs, out of my province, or that are beyond the sphere, in which I suppose, I was designed originally, by Congress, to move.*——Such, I imagine, is the arrangement of Hospital affairs, in Canada, and the undertaking to supply the Surgeons there with what is necessary for a General Hospital, without fresh instructions, or more ample power than I now have, either from the Congress or Commander in Chief, as my commission directs me to look to them, for orders.

I wait, impatiently, for an order from Congress, to impower me to demand such a proportion of the Continental medicines, left in the care of Messieurs De Lancy and Smith, as they may think fit to allot for this department. In determining that proportion, they will please to consider (if we can trust to Dr. Lind's account) that there is not an article of medicine in Canada, in the hands of any Surgeon on that expedition.

June 26, 1776. Since writing the above, Dr. Potts having received a supply of medicines, from the General Hospital store, Dr. Lind has set off with General Gates and him, for Canada.

    I remain, with great esteem,
     SIR,
      Your most obedient,
       and very humble servant,
        JOHN MORGAN.

☞ *This*

☞ *This may certify, that I remember to have heard* Doctor MORGAN *read the foregoing letter, in July, 1776, together with several others, upon the subject of the General Hospital and Regimental Surgeons, all inculcating the immediate necessity of putting them upon a proper footing.*

JOHN WARREN, Hospital Surgeon.

BEFORE I proceed to exhibit a copy of the next letter, which I wrote to Congress, it will not be improper to inform the reader of the occasion of it.

Having been returned from Philadelphia, about a fortnight after my conference with the Medical Committee of Congress, in which I had set forth my insufficiency, without farther powers and instructions, to answer all the calls daily made on me, in an extensive and unsettled department; and, having received no orders or directions from Congress, all this while, in answer to my application for that purpose: A powerful fleet and army from Great-Britain, intended for the reduction of New-York, being likewise already arrived on the coast; and having prepared every thing in my department, that was in my power, I then considered the unsettled state of the regimental Surgeons. In order to bring them, by degrees, into greater regularity, and to make them more useful in case of action, as many of them had but newly entered the service, and most of them, from want of experience, were yet novices in the duties of a military Surgeon, I thought it adviseable to give them some instructions, which might open their minds to a sense of what duty was required of them, as regimental Surgeons, in time of action, which it could not be supposed, was very distant. I, thereupon, drew up the following directions, and communicated them to the General.—He approved of them in the orders of the day; and commanded the several Surgeons of Regiments to wait upon me for copies, and to regulate themselves according to the proposed plan.

Each Surgeon was allowed a copy, and commonly, at the same time, I gave him an order on the Apothecary, of the General Hospital, for a medicine chest, for every Battalion, which he also obtained, if he was not already provided, together with a number of bandages, and tourniquets, and a quantity of lint, tow, and old linnen, for chirurgical dressings.

A COPY OF THE

ORDER and INSTRUCTIONS,

Given to the REGIMENTAL SURGEONS,

In case of ACTION.

New-York, July 3, 1776.

IT is proposed by the Director-General, and ordered by his Excellency the Commander in Chief, That the Regimental Surgeons and Mates may be the better prepared for the discharge of their duty, in case of action, to hold themselves in immediate and constant readiness for service; and, in the first place, to make a return to the Director General of the Hospital, of their names and stations, and of the instruments and bandages, &c. they have at hand, agreeable to the following FORM, viz.

A

A REGIMENTAL Return of Surgeon's Instruments and Bandages, &c. now in Readiness for immediate Service, belonging to Colonel ————'s Regiment, in Brigadier General ————'s Brigade, encamped at ————, July 3, 1776.

Names of the Surgeon and Mate, and the dates of their commission.	Instruments fit for use.	Number & kind of Bandages, &c. Ligatures, &c.	Old Linnen and other Implements.
Surgeon. Mate.	Amputating Instruments. Trepanning, do. Incision knives. Pocket Instruments. Bullet Forceps. Crooked needles Strait do. Pins.	Simple Rollers. Double do. Foliated bandages. Splints. Tourniquets. Ligatures. Tape. Thread.	Quantity of old Linnen or weight of Rags. Weight or Quantity of Lint, Tow, &c. Spunge. (Place to be signed by the Surgeon.)

AS the General Hospital will not admit of the Hospital Surgeons and Mates being divided, or detached from the places where the General Hospital is fixed, and may require occasional assistance from the Regimental Surgeons, in case of many wounded being sent to it, in order that the Hospital and Regimental Surgeons may concur, at this time, to render their mutual services more effectual and extensive, the following regulations are to be observed for the present, and till any change of circumstances may require an alteration.

Part of the General Hospital is now fixed at Long-Island, for the reception of sick and wounded persons, whose cases may require it; which JOHN WARREN, Esq; Surgeon in the General Hospital, is appointed to superintend and direct, with the assistance of three
Hospital

Hospital Mates, and such other Regimental Surgeons and Mates, belonging to that part of the army stationed at Long-Island, as may be required. In case of evident necessity, arising from an attempt being made on Fort Defiance, (afterwards called Fort Washington,) two of the Hospital Mates, with Doctor M'Henry, now at Montresor Island, and whom he is to superintend and direct, are to repair to that post, with a proper assortment of instruments and bandages. The remainder of the Surgeons and Mates of the General Hospital, are to continue at King's-College, and New-York Hospital, for the reception and care of such wounded as are sent to them, from what ever part. It being the duty of the Regimental Surgeons and Mates, in case of action, in the field, to attend the Corps to which they belong, in order to dress the wounded in battle; they are to take post in the rear of the troops engaged in action, at the distance of three, four, or five hundred yards, behind some convenient hill, if at hand, there to dress the wounded, who require to be dressed, on or near the field of battle. If the Regiment or Corps to which they belong, are engaged within a fort, or lines thrown up for defence, that fort or place of defence, is then the proper station for the Regimental Surgeons: But as a Regiment may be divided, and distributed into different posts, so as to render it impracticable for the Regimental Surgeon and Mate, belonging to that Regiment, to be near some parts of their Corps, it is necessary that, an account of the number of Surgeons and Mates, in any Brigade, or any division of the army, that occupies one or more detached posts, be taken, and delivered to the Commanding Officer of said posts or division. It is to be considered as the duty of each Regimental Surgeon and Mate respectively, wherever stationed, to regard himself, as having a joint charge of the whole Brigade, with the rest of the Surgeons of that Brigade, rather than as if his care was to be confined only to those officers and soldiers who are of the Regiment to

which

which he belongs. It muſt unavoidably happen, at times, that both officers and ſoldiers may be wounded in action, and their particular Surgeons be elſewhere employed, ſo as not to be able to attend them. The amputation of a limb, or performance of any capital operation, cannot well take place in the heat of a briſk action: It is ſeldom poſſible, or requiſite. What the Surgeon has chiefly to attend to, in caſes of perſons being much wounded in the field of battle, is to ſtop any flux of blood, either by tourniquet, ligature, lint and compreſs, or a ſuitable bandage, as the caſe may require; to remove any extraneous body from the wound; to reduce fractured bones; to apply proper dreſſings to wounds; taking care on the one hand, not to bind up the parts too tightly, ſo as to injure the blood's circulation, increaſe inflammation, and excite a fever; or ſo looſely, as to endanger the wounds bleeding afreſh, or to allow broken bones, after they are properly ſet, to be again diſplaced. The wounded being thus dreſſed by the Regimental Surgeons, are next to be removed to the neareſt Hoſpital belonging to the Brigade, or to the General Hoſpital, as may be moſt convenient.

As the General Hoſpital may at times, be fully crouded with ſick perſons, or in the time of action, ſo many wounded may be ſent there, as to require a greater number of hands, than that part of the General Hoſpital, where many of the wounded are ſent, is furniſhed with, it may be abſolutely neceſſary for the ſuperintending Surgeon, beſides the proportion allowed him, from the General Hoſpital, to call for the aſſiſtance of a number of Surgeons and Mates, from the Brigade, diviſion or part of the army where he is, either before an engagement, or, when the number of wounded perſons ſent to him becomes very great, making ſuch aſſiſtance needful. For this purpoſe, he is to apply to the Commander of that Brigade, or part of the army, who is hereby ordered to ſend him as many Regimental Surgeons

geons and Mates, for that purpose, as are required, and can be spared from their posts.

To prevent confusion, and that the Regimental Surgeons may know the better what part of duty is expected from them, some one, at least, of the Surgeons, especially those fixed at out posts, are directed, as soon as possible, to call upon and arrange matters, in time, with the Hospital Surgeons nearest at hand, in behalf of the Brigade, or Corps acting together, that no disorder may arise, in time of action, for want of so necessary a precaution. The Regimental Surgeons ought to call on the officers of the Corps to which they belong, to settle with them, what persons are to be employed in carrying off the wounded, and for a supply of wheel-barrows, or other more convenient biers, for conveying them from the field of battle, to the place appointed for reception of the wounded, or General Hospital. Each Regimental Surgeon and Mate ought to have a portable box, with suitable divisions for containing his lint, bandages, instruments, and other implements of Surgery, which ought to be well provided with every necessary.

In applying a common tourniquet to stop the flow of blood, from any principal artery in a limb, till it can be otherwise properly secured, care must be taken not to twist it too tightly about the limb; and to prevent the tourniquet from slipping, so as to endanger a fresh loss of blood, it must be fastened with a ligature of thread or tape.

JOHN MORGAN, Director-General.

IN consequence of the foregoing plan and orders, some reports were made, although they came in but slowly. Near a fortnight passed over, before I received them from more than fifteen Regimental Surgeons: It is to be ascribed, if not to that backwardness which the Regimental Surgeons ever shewed to complying with
General

General Orders, perhaps, to a confcious fhame of being entirely deftitute of any neceffary articles, but what they had been previoufly indulged to draw from the General Hofpital: Some of them, whom I afterwards met, and inquired into the caufe of their neglect, confeffed this to be the truth. As my intention in defiring thofe reports to be made to me, was, to lay them before the General and Congrefs, with remarks on their infufficiency, that the Medical Committee might be incited to ufe more diligence, than heretofore, to fall on fome meafures for fupplying the Regimental Surgeons, with every neceffary to qualify them for greater ufefulnefs in their ftation. I drew up, from the feparate reports delivered to me, one general return of the ftate of the abovementioned fifteen Regiments. All the inftruments were reported to be private property, and amounted to fix fets of amputating inftruments, two of trepanning ditto, fifteen cafes of pocket inftruments, feventy-five crooked, and fix ftrait needles. Amongft the whole fifteen Surgeons, there were only four fcalpels or incifion knives, for dilating of wounds, or any other purpofe; three pair of forceps, for extracting bullets; half a paper and feventy pins; and but few bandages, ligatures or tourniquets, and as little old linnen, lint or tow, but what they had procured from the General Hofpital; and only two ounces of fpunge in all. Amazing deficiency for fifteen Surgeons, and as many Mates!

Upon inquiry how they could think of marching with their Regiments, without providing, at leaft, old linnen for dreffings; or of joining the army, without the neceffary inftruments, as, if ever they reflected at all, they muft be fenfible of the impropriety of fo doing, and of its being much eafier for each man, to procure thofe articles, within the fphere of his acquaintance, connexions or neighbourhood, than to obtain them in an army, in general, deftitute of neceffary fupplies, of what was not to be procured in America, but with great difficulty.

ficulty. Their conſtant anſwer was, whenever they applied to their ſuperior officers for thoſe things, they were always told, they would be furniſhed with every thing they wanted, ſo ſoon as they ſhould have joined the army. Upon being informed that I had only a ſufficiency of thoſe articles for the uſe of the General Hoſpital, and that I would by no means unfurniſh it, to ſupply them, they appeared quite confounded, and expreſſed great uneaſineſs, at having no proper eſtabliſhment; and ſaid, they knew not how, or where to obtain the neceſſary articles, to be any ways uſeful in the army, if I did not aſſiſt them.

As I was not ignorant of the many inconveniencies, under which they had hitherto laboured, from a want of attention in the Congreſs to relieve, or place them on a better footing, and as I felt for their diſtreſs, I aſſured them of my readineſs to aſſiſt them, all in my power, conſiſtently with my proper duty, and the orders I had, or ſhould receive from Congreſs. I adviſed them to meet in a body; to converſe on the matter with each other; and then chuſe one or more Deputies, from each Brigade, to ſtate their helpleſs ſituation, and pray for relief; in which I was willing to ſecond their application, with all the influence of which I was maſter.

As they complained much of not being allowed proper Regimental Hoſpitals, and, as I had, in oppoſition to what always appeared to me to be the ſentiments, both of the Congreſs and General, ever uniformly given it as my opinion, that Regimental Surgeons and Regimental Hoſpitals, under proper regulations, and due ſubordination to the General Hoſpital, might be very uſeful, I took that matter under my conſideration. I likewiſe drew up a memorial, and propoſals, to be ſhewn to the General, for his approbation and concurrence, to be laid before Congreſs. At the ſame time, I penned for the uſe of the Regimental Surgeons, a form, and directions for keeping a proper regiſter of the ſick, and

for

for making every kind of necessary returns of sick, provisions, &c. also tables of the various kinds of diet, used in the General Hospital, as an example for themselves, to copy after, under the heads of full diet, half diet, low diet, milk diet and fever diet, with the method of calculating the differences betwixt these, and the amount of the well rations; to enable them to draw the value of the difference, whether in cash or refreshments, but for the use of the sick only: And I shewed them a list of what instruments, bandages, ligatures, lint, tow, old linnen and other articles, I esteemed necessary for a Regiment; which I shall subjoin to the substance of the memorial and petition to Congress, and the proposals I had sketched out for their consideration.

At the first meeting I had with them, by appointment, to confer on these several particulars, before I produced the papers referred to, I addressed them in these words, which I had written, and of which I kept the original.

ADDRESS to the SURGEONS.

Gentlemen,

I HAVE, with all the care and attention in my power, taken into consideration, the state of the Regimental Surgeons, with a view to getting them provided with Regimental Hospitals, and pointing out the means for their being, in future, supplied with the usual requisites, for the more easy, more regular, and more extensive discharge of the duties annexed to their station. To answer this end, I have considered what is within our power, as matters now stand, and what we are to aim at, for further improvement; and have, by a train of reflexions on the subject, been led, in the first place, to propose certain regulations which appear to me to be both salutary and practicable, if they meet with your concurrence;

concurrence; for which I shall submit them to your hearing and strictures, for correction and amendment. If we can agree in them, it will be one step gained, and may serve as a foundation, on which to proceed, in smoothing every difficulty that may still remain, towards forming a more perfect plan, or model of œconomy, in the conducting of Military Hospitals, and providing for the sick and wounded.

The next step which I apprehend we have to take, is to apply to Congress for an immediate supply of chirurgical instruments and bandages, for the Regimental Surgeons, and for its approbation of the proposed regulations, as well as that of the Commander in Chief; that those regulations may have a proper authority to rest upon, for their sanction and support; and, 3dly, to suggest such others, as may be still more useful, in future, should the continuance of the war make any further regulations necessary.

July, 1776.   J. M.

The MEMORIAL of the REGIMENTAL SURGEONS, To CONGRESS.

Sets forth, THAT when troops were assembled in haste, at the first breaking out of the war, Regimental Surgeons were appointed to accompany them, provided with medicine chests, from the different parts of the country, where they were raised, at a Colonial expence.—That when it became a common cause of the whole continent, and provision was made, by Congress, for the care of the sick and wounded of the army, by the establishment of a General

ral Hospital, with a Director General, four Surgeons and twenty Mates, there was no mention of the Regimental Surgeons and Mates, nor any provision made for them, either of medicines, instruments, or other necessaries; yet they were kept in pay.—That, in this situation, although it might be presumed the Hospital Surgeons and Mates, appointed to take care of the sick and wounded, were scarcely sufficient to attend so great a number of patients as an unhealthy season, or an active campaign might produce; yet the Regimental Surgeons and Mates, for want of a suitable provision, must, in their present situation, be very useless; although they were so much more numerous than the Hospital Surgeons and Mates, and always professed an ardent desire of being properly employed, and of answering the design of their appointment.—That not knowing where else to look for relief, they had applied to the Director-General, who assured them of his inclination to serve them; but having no orders to issue out supplies to them, and it being unusual for Regimental Surgeons to depend upon the General Hospital for all they wanted, he had advised them to make application to the Commander in Chief, or Congress, for establishing a proper method to obtain supplies, promising to second their applications, with the warmest representations from himself —That it was with his advice, the present memorial was drawn up, to lay before Congress.—That he had given them several meetings, and a set of proposals were agreed upon, as regulations, provided they met with the approbation of Congress, which were inclosed for consideration; praying for such relief on the premisses, as to the wisdom of Congress should seem meet.

REGULATIONS

REGULATIONS proposed by the Director-General of the Hospital; and agreed upon with the Regimental Surgeons, to be laid before CONGRESS FOR THEIR DETERMINATION upon them.

1st. THAT the Regimental Surgeons apply to the Quarter-Master-General, and obtain from him, or the Barrack-Master, by an order from him, some proper quarters convenient for the situation of each Brigade, by the name of Regimental or Brigade Hospitals.

2d. That the said Hospitals be furnished from the Quarter-Master General's department, with necessary utensils and Hospital furniture, according to a list of enumerated particulars.

3d. That the Regimental Surgeons be supplied, in future, by Continental Druggists, with medicines, instruments and old linnen for bandages, and necessary dressings.

4th. That they shall report to the Director-General, or Surgeons of the General Hospital, all such sick patients of their Regiments, who are proper objects; making use of every possible precaution, to guard against crowding the Hospital with putrid cases, that require fresh air for recovery of the sick, least hospital, malignant, or pestilential diseases be excited, to the great devastation and ruin of the army.

5th. That they shall keep an exact register of the sick, in which they shall enter the names of the patients, the companies to which they belong, the disorders they labour under, the times of their admission, or being considered as unfit for duty; with the times and event of their diseases, of recovery, death, or dismission.

6th. That they make proper reports, extracted from said

said register, to accompany every person they recommend to the General hospital, with an account of the patients case, and previous treatment, and what cloathing is sent with each patient, certified by the Surgeon or Mate, and signed also by a commissioned officer.

7. That they make daily returns to the Quarter-Master or Adjutant of the regiment; of the sick belonging to that regiment, who are unfit for duty, whether remaining under their own care, or sent to the General hospital, that no soldiers may be exempted from duty, as sick men, that are not borne on the Doctor's list; and that no rations be drawn for them, amongst the effective men, whilst they are drawn for with the sick, whether in the General or regimental hospitals.

8. That they make weekly returns of the sick from their registers, both in the General hospital, and regimental, or brigade hospitals, as well to the Director-General, as to the Commandant of the regiment or brigade, that a true state of the sick of the whole army may be made out, to lay before the Commander in chief, and to be transmitted to Congress, weekly.

9. That agreeable to the sick list returned to the Director General, the regimental Surgeons be intitled to draw from the General hospital, for the sick remaining under their care, any articles they may chuse, agreeable to the various diet tables made use of for the patients of the General hospital; and whatever other stores or refreshments they chuse, with which the General hospital is supplied, to the full amount of their rations. If they require more from the General hospital, the sick are to be sent to the General hospital

10. That the Colonels of regiments be allowed to draw monies for defraying any extraordinary or incidental charges of regimental hospitals, and for such articles as are not to be got in the store of the General hospital, nor in the commissarial or Quarter-Master's department, and an account of the disbursements to be settled, with the weekly or monthly abstract of the regiment.

I That

11. That the state of the several regimental or brigade hospitals, of the sick, and of the medicine chests, be subject to examination, from time to time, of the Director-General or such hospital Surgeons as he shall appoint to that duty.

12 That in all things, not particularly ascertained in these regulations, the usage of the British and other armies be followed, till otherwise directed, as far as is consistent with the good of the service.

THE foregoing, as nearly as I can recollect, is the substance of the memorial and proposals agreed upon. I remember the import well. If it differs materially, it is in the power of the regimental Surgeons to shew the difference, by printing the orginial papers. I gave my drafts thereof to them, which they considered, and proposed some alterations, that I convinced them could not be adopted. They acquiesced in the reasons I gave. I then made some small emendations in the copies, which, with the alterations and interlineations in my own hand writing, are still in possession of Doctor Story, late Surgeon of Colonel Little's regiment; one of those who were present at the conference. It is not long since I called on him for a copy of both the memorial and proposals. He promised to let me have them; but afterwards, being void of honour, broke his word, for which he would assign no other reason, than that he did not know what use I should make of them to his disadvantage, though I told him, before my design of publishing them, and that I wished to have the original papers before me, or exact copies of them, that I might not be charged with any misrepresentation to the publick; which, by communicating them to me, it was in his power to prevent. But this is not the only instance of meanness, joined with insolence of behaviour, which I have had occasion to publish to the world, and which I have yet to produce, to delineate the character of this shameless man.

LETTER SECOND.

New-York, July, 1776.

To Messieurs
SAMUEL ADAMS, Esquire,

And the rest of the Medical Committee of Congress.

GENTLEMEN,

HAVING put the General hospital on a good footing at New-York, and provided it with a pretty considerable stock of what it may stand in need of (as a general hospital) I have thought it my duty to turn my attention to the regimental surgeons. Their situation, ever since I have been in the army, has been such as to require a great deal of regulation.

If I were to confine myself to the true and proper business of Director General of the hospital, I should have very little concerns with them as regimental Surgeons, according to the plan of the British establishment. It would be principally confined to the receiving such sick from them, into the General hospital, as they could not take care of themselves; to assist in the examination of such as offered themselves candidates for the places of Surgeons and Mates; and to give orders to them to supply themselves with proper medicinal chests, for each regiment, and all the instruments and implements necessary for them to be provided with, and see it done. The making provision of those articles should depend on themselves; but they ought to be supplied with the means, whether by an allowance of money adequate to the provision, or by a stoppage from the mens pay.

I found them, upon enquiry, destitute of every article, whether of medicines, instruments, bandages or other implements of surgery; and not knowing where to provide what was necessary, or who to look to for assistance. With

With a view to promote the service all that lay in my power, I have attempted to bring them together, to examine into the state of their wants; to point out what they ought to be furnished with; to direct them where to look for supplies; and to bring them under some proper regulations.

To answer these several purposes, I began, by requesting the General to issue out orders for each Surgeon, to make a return of what medicines he had on hand. To my sorrow, I must say it, excepting two or three Regiments, the stock of all the Regiments at Cambridge put together, would scarcely have made one good chest. I procured all I could get at Boston, and have, from thence, and from some purchases of shops at Salem, and some articles I got at Newport, Norwich and New-York, furnished Regimental chests to all the Regimental Surgeons, who have hitherto applied, to the amount of near twenty; and am still furnishing all the new regiments that daily come in.

In the next place, I sketched out a plan of conduct, for the Surgeons of Regiments in case of action, of which the General approved, and gave out in orders, that they should attend, and take directions from me, on that head *. At the same time, I desired a report to be delivered in, of their Surgeons instruments, and bandages fit for use, agreeable to a form given them for the purpose. Fifteen Regimental Surgeons made their returns accordingly; from which I have drawn up one general return, to shew the amount: I suppose them to be, at least, as well provided as any others, that have neglected to pay due attention to the order; and do find, that the Regiments now coming in have Surgeons and Mates, but not one article of medicine, or any thing in the way of Surgery, but all depend on me for supplies.

I have sketched out, what in my opinion, every Regiment ought to be supplied with, in the way of instruments.

* See that plan and orders of July 3d, Page 54.

ments. By comparing this sketch, with the returns made for fifteen Regiments, the great want of every thing essential to them, as Surgeons, will be evident.

To make amends for their defect, I am well off in the Gen. Hospital, except in a few particulars. I have provided 10,000 bandages, have some hundred old sheets, and a stock of medicines (tho' unassorted;) I have of capital instruments nearly enough for Hospital use. But, in the mean time, what is to become of the Regimental Surgeons? Should I divide my stores amongst them, they would be dissipated, and ourselves left destitute. To observe a medium, I have ordered to be issued from the General Hospital stores, 60 bandages, 2 sheets, 4 tourniquets, a quantity of lint and tow, and a chest of medicines, out of what I have collected with the assistance of the Hospital Surgeons and Mates, who bare no proportion, in number, to the Regimental Surgeons and Mates, (there being, perhaps, 40 Regiments here,) reserving the rest to supply that particular part of the army which may stand in most need: But of instruments, I have none to spare, and I begin to want some capital medicines.—Moreover, symptoms of a putrid fever begin to appear.

In this situation, I have called many of the Regimental Surgeons together; have had a conference with them; desired a deputation from each Brigade; have given them a plan of regulations for Regimental Hospitals, and a form of a memorial, or representation to Congress. They all look to me, for supplies of every thing they want: I have no authority for that purpose. It is contrary to my judgment to supply them with all they want. To prove this, I refer you to all who know any thing of the matter. I refer you to Dr. Bass, in Philadelphia, who knows these matters as well as any man: I refer you to a copy of a letter, on this subject, from a man of experience, which I enclose *. I must not, I durst not transgress orders, or exceed my
line

* See the next letter.

line of duty more than disobey, or go contrary to them. It is the same thing. I call for orders. I shall shrink from no fatigue: Say what is my duty, and to the best of my power, I will obey: But leave me not without orders. Every General, every Colonel of a Regiment, every surgeon in the army think I have full power, and ample instructions, and know not where to apply for the relief of their men, if sick or wounded, and needing uncommon supplies, if I cannot afford them. It is a cruel situation. My errand to Philadelphia was to represent these things; to settle the channels of supply; to obtain sufficient means, or authority sufficient to procure them. I am bound to a spot: Scarcely could I obtain permission to leave this place, for a few days, to come to Philadelphia, and lay these matters before you.

Again, I am pressed on the side of Canada. I have wrote pressingly on this subject. I have sent you a letter from Dr. Potts. He says, there are 3000 sick, coming to Albany. I have not received the least answer, or instruction from Congress; nor can I give any assistance to that part of the army, without orders or power. Let them give me orders. whether limited or ample, they shall be obeyed. I will answer for my conduct. But do not make me nominal Gen. Director, and leave me, at the same time, a destitute, a helpless one. I have requested my proportion of the medicines in the hands of Messieurs Delaney and Smith, to be kept sacred, untouched, subject to my order: Perhaps it is too late to repeat the request.

I will inclose this, with a plan observed by the British, in the conduct of their General and Regimental Hospitals; and papers to illustrate and support what I have written; sufficient to compile some rules, or form some orders. I beg instruments may be sent us, particularly amputating; crooked needles and spunge. The enemy are at hand: The campaign is opening: I have done all my limited power will allow. I hope,

though

though late, almost too late, yet that it is not altogether so, either to receive power, instructions, or means to regulate the affairs of my department. I have done my duty, in giving the necessary information for what is connected with it, and in preparing for the faithful discharge of my trust. I now rest the matter on your determinations, being, with all possible regard,

Gentlemen,

Your most dutiful and obedient Servant,

JOHN MORGAN.

Norwalk, February 12, 1777.

☞ *I remember to have heard Doctor* MORGAN *read this letter, about the month of July last, with several others on the subject, to shew what he was then doing, to put the Regimental Surgeons on some better footing.*

W. EUSTIS, Surgeon in the Gen. Hosp.

THE only letter I received from Mr. Adams, is dated August 5, in which he says: "I have received several letters from you, which I should have sooner acknowledged, if I could have found leisure. I took, however, the necessary steps, to have what you requested, effected in Congress."

THE letter from a gentleman originally consulted by Congress, on the establishment of the General Hospital, mentioned in the note, page 69; being the same with that to which I referred General WASHINGTON, in my memorial page 6, is as follows:

To Doctor JOHN MORGAN,

Director-General of the *Continental Hospitals*,

At CAMBRIDGE, &c.

Philadelphia, February 24, 1776.

SIR,

LAST week, I received yours, of the 1st inst. The Regimental Surgeons were never allowed medicines from the Hospital, unless their own happened to be expended, from being long encamped in a part of the country, where none could possibly be got: And to prevent their being out of medicines, as much as possible, previous to their taking the field, their medicine chests were always examined, by order of the Commander in Chief, by the officers of the Hospital; to see they were provided with their proper stores for the service they were going upon, and a report was made to the Commander in Chief, accordingly.

When it was found proper to deliver them medicines, they were no more than might serve them till they went into quarters, or could be supplied from any neighbouring place. As to any other stores, I never knew them once thought of, or demanded.

Every Regiment had an Hospital to itself, for slight cases, which the Surgeon and his Mates took care of; the charges of which were always defrayed by the Regiment.

The medicinal and chirurgical stores for the Hospital were, for every campaign, fixed and ordered, the preceeding winter, by the Physicians, Apothecaries and Surgeons, in a joint consultation.

To give you our long lists of medicines, &c. (" *on any expedition last war, as you request,*") would avail you little at present, as many of the articles are not to be had; nay, I am certain, one half of them might, at any time, be left out: When you come to town, you shall see them; They are too long for a letter.

We always made our own bandages, splints, tourniquets, &c. from old linnen, leather, &c. we sent out on purpose. We had never less than five hundred old sheets, and two or three hundred skins came out at once, which the Hospital Mates made into the different kinds of bandages, &c. in common use.

General Gates can inform you, that the estimates I gave in for the Hospital, including the pay of the officers, were ten thousand pounds for the first six months, for ten thousand men, and in the same proportion for a larger number.

I am, Sir,

Your most humble Servant, &c.

The following is a report of what instruments, bandages, ligatures, tow, &c. a Regimental Surgeon and Mate ought to have in readiness, for service, in case of action, for a Regiment, consisting of a thousand men; and so in proportion.

Instruments for Surgeon and Mate.	Bandages, &c.	Linnen, &c.
A set of amputating Instruments, consisting of at least	Of Bandages, Rollers, &c. of various kinds, at least 300.	Six pair of old sheets, or rags equivalent, for compresses, &c.
A large knife,	One or two dozen sets of splints,	
a saw with two blades,	a dozen common tour-	Lint, 2 or 3 pounds at least,
a catline,		12 crooked

12 crooked needles, and a screw tourniquet. A case of 6 incision knives, 2 sets of pocket instruments, 4 bullet forcipes, an artery forceps, 2 dozen strait needles, a paper of pins, a case of lancets.	niquets, 3 ounces of thread, for ligatures, a peice or two of inch wide tape, 16 or 18 inches square of sadler's-leather, and a piece of sadler's inch wide girting. Bandages, tourniquets, splints, &c. should be made by the Surgeon and Mate.	6 pounds of fine tow 6 ounces of spunge. J. M. D. G.

IN the same packet, with the foregoing letter to the Medical Committee of Congress, page 67; I inclosed a variety of papers for their confideration, namely, copies of the instructions given to the Regimental Surgeons July the third, page 54; of their intended memorial to Congress, page 62; of the regulations proposed and agreed upon with them, for the allowance of Regimental Hospitals, page 64; of the preceeding letter, from a gentleman at Philadelphia, very conversant in the subject, to shew what were the usages and customs of the General Hospital, in the British service; and particularly to declare what kind of stores, and under what circumstances, the Regimental Surgeons were allowed to draw from the General Hospital in that service, page 72; and of the foregoing report of instruments and bandages necessary for every Regiment, page 73; together with copies of the different diet tables, and other regulations of the General Hospital. These were severally indorsed and numbered, being calculated for the purpose, and intended to answer the promise I had made his EXCELLENCY GENERAL WASHINGTON, in the beginning of my letter to him, of March, page 32; by explaining the nature, both of the General and Regimental Hospitals;

pointing

pointing out the uses and proper government of each; their separate and distinct designs; the means of supplying the Regimental, and rendering them more useful, by placing them in a due subordination to the General, Hospitals. I did not doubt the works being acceptable, both to the General and the Congress, as it might be supposed, they were not much versed themselves, in these matters; with which, however, it was necessary for the good of the service, they should be acquainted.

To understand the better what were the uses of the copies of the different diet tables, and of other regulations of the General Hospital, which accompanied my letter to the Medical Committee of Congress; and to demonstrate, at the same time, what pains I was at, to introduce method and exactness into every branch of the department entrusted to my care, as I have omitted to mention the particulars before, it will be very proper to take notice, in this place, of the steps I had taken for that purpose, when at Cambridge.

So soon after my arrival in the army as to have been able to take a review of the state, in which the General Hospital then was, I appointed a meeting of the Hospital Surgeons, to take under consideration the proper steps to be pursued for the better government of the Hospital. I, therefore, in the first place, shewed them my commission, with the instructions from Congress for the establishment of the General Hospital; I explained to them my idea, of the duties of the several officers, and gave them a form of the various returns which I expected to be made, on the various occasions of the Hospital. I laid before them the different diet tables that were in use, in the General Hospital of the British army, last war, as well as those in the different Hospitals of London and Westminster, with all the regulations observed, in each distinct part and office, for the government of St. Thomas's Hospital, which I had procured at the time I was pupil there, under the celebrated

brated Physicians, Milner, Akenside and Russell, and brought with me to the army.

With these regulations before us, compared with the nature and diseases of the climate, and those incident to an army, with the provisions of the country, and manner of living, as well as the nature of our establishment, several sets of rules were drawn up for the better regulating of our own Hospitals, and particularly for ascertaining, and enforcing the duties of the Surgeons, the Mates, the Apothecaries, the Stewarts, the Matron and Nurses, the Waiters and Attendants; and also rules for the observance of the Patients. It would protract this piece, to too great a length, were I to insert them here: I therefore content myself, with taking notice, that the perfecting them was a work of time and of mature reflexion, which would do no discredit to any of the gentlemen that were concerned in the performance, were I to publish them at large. And I must, to do justice to this task enjoined them, which was submitted to my own corrections, observe, that it was the means of introducing that exactitude in duty, and that better œconomy and discipline into the General Hospital, that were wanted, as might be naturally expected; by means of which, all the proper business of the Hospital was afterwards conducted with more regularity, ease and satisfaction to the officers, and greater benefit and advantages to the patients; all which were much wanted, in all the transactions I have ever had with the Regimental Surgeons.

This I thought a proper employment for a Director General, and deserving the attention of the Congress and Commander in Chief. I therefore dispatched them to the General, by return of one of his servants, sent to engage me to come to Head-Quarters, for his perusal at first, and then to be forwarded to Congress; hoping he would be pleased to second my letter to Congress, with some representation from himself, of the necessity of adopting these, or some other regulations
to

to answer the intention, for which these papers might serve as a proper foundation on which to proceed. They were accompanied with a note to Colonel Reed the Adjutant-General, in which I wrote as follows:

SIR,

I imagine the annexed regulations, &c. for the establishment, management and supplies of the Regimental Hospitals, will be of great use in the army, and tend to remove the frequent complaints of Regimental Surgeons, respecting the want of some better provision for the sick under their care, and enable them to discharge their duty with more CHEARFULNESS, and ADVANTAGE to the service.

They are submitted with the Memorial &c. to Congress, to General Washington's perusal, if he has time to consider them, for his approbation. It will appear on reading them, that those, or some such regulations, are much wanted, and cannot take place, unless they have his sanction in General Orders.

Perhaps you may have so much leisure as to examine the several enclosed papers, and communicate the substance of them to the General, if he is not sufficiently disengaged to look over them, himself. I intend, agreeeable to your desire, to be at Head-Quarters early, to come at two o'clock, that there may be some time for conversing on this subject, before dinner."

I requested, that after the General had satisfied himself in respect to the contents of these papers, they might be forwarded with his dispatches to Congress.

WHEN next I had an opportunity of speaking with the General, and supposed he might have acquainted himself with the purport and design of those papers, I took the liberty of asking his opinion of them. He had been greatly hurried, as I could perceive by the number of applicants to himself, on a variety of business

ness, of different departments. His answer, therefore, was such as might be expected, couched in the following interrogatory : How can you think, I have time to read over such a bundle of papers ? I told him I was sensible of his situation, and how precious his time was ; that the reason of my troubling him with so much writing, was that he might not be interrupted by long consultations, though on the most necessary matters; but be able to make himself master of the subject, when most at leisure to consider it, with the means before him : I informed him as briefly as possible, of the general contents, and what I had written to the Adjutant General, in whose abilities he placed great confidence ; and concluded with a request, that if he should not have leisure shortly, to read them over himself, that he would refer them to Colonel Reed, or any other person he chose, to give him an account of them, that some orders might issue in consequence : They related to important matters, and nothing could be done in them, without his orders, on which he let me know, that I should hear from him soon, on the business they were intended to recommend to his notice.

I think it was that very day, the resolves of Congress, July 17th, came to hand, and were communicated to me, of which I obtained a certified copy from the Adjutant-General, and another, about four days afterwards from Colonel Robert H. Harrison, Secretary to the General, which bears date July 26, 1776.

In the mean time, the Regimental Surgeons, who were impatient to know the General's mind, that they might take their measures accordingly, for making a personal application to himself, which they judged would answer as well as applying to Congress ; or for forwarding the memorial and petition to Congress, as might appear most suitable, on knowing his mind ; were made acquainted with the beforementioned resolves. These resolves produced a general disgust in the Regimental Surgeons, as they anticipated, and might prevent

vent the success of any application to Congress at that time; and cut them off from all present hopes of carrying into execution, their favourite scheme of having Regimental Hospitals under their own management, furnished and supplied to their wishes; and from the expectation of handling public monies.

The chagrin and bitterness of spirit which they manifested on this occasion, is inexpressible; and every mean artifice that could be devised, was carried into execution by some of them, to counteract, and, if possible, to evade those resolves. They gave proof indeed, that, for the infamy of it, deserves to be recorded, to what degrees of weakness, blindness and folly, men destitute of the principles of honour and honesty will be transported, by a false pride, and the disappointment of secret and ambitious views, when they prefer the gratification of their own desires, however unjust, to the interest of the cause they are engaged to promote, if opposed to each other. But I shall defer giving the particulars, till I have first communicated a letter, which with a view to serve those ungrateful men all in my power, I wrote to General Washington, and is as follows:

New-York, July 25, 1776.

To his Excellency

GENERAL WASHINGTON,

SIR,

THE Congress having come into a number of resolves respecting the General Hospital, &c. I find that one of them, as it now stands, gives great uneasiness to the Regimental Surgeons. It is that which prohibits them from drawing upon the Hospital of their department for any stores, except medicines and instruments; and orders, that when any sick person shall

require

require other stores, they shall be received into the General Hospital, and the rations of the said sick persons be stopped, so long as they are in the said Hospital.

The Regimental Surgeons seem to think, if this resolve should remain as it now stands, without any palliative construction in favor of supplying the sick, under their care, with necessary articles of diet, &c. (for no provision is made by any of these resolves for changing the diet of the sick, and their rations would be very improper diet) they have nothing left, but immediately to order the whole of their sick into the General Hospital. What would be the consequence ? Instead of about three hundred, which is the present number of the sick in the General Hospital, it would immediately amount to two thousand or upwards, and the numbers increase every day. But where we shall get room for them, is the difficulty; and in case of an action, and many persons being wounded, that difficulty would increase : The General Hospital would be crowded, and the Regimental Surgeons, who profess their ardent desire of being usefully employed, would complain of having nothing to do. But what is the worst part of it, as the dysentery, and fevers of a putrid kind now prevail ; the crowding so many together into the General Hospital, would certainly engender a malignant, pestilential fever, that would threaten the ruin of the army.

These difficulties, in my opinion, might for the present, be got over in one of these two ways, the choice of which is left to your Excellency.

The first, is by adopting a set of regulations, drawn up and agreed upon, betwixt the Regimental Surgeons and myself, (if it met with your Excellency's approbation,) and which I laid before your Excellency, a fortnight ago, for your consideration.

Otherwise, let the Regimental Surgeons be suffered to keep such men in their own Regimental Hospitals, under their own care, whose cases would endanger the spreading of putrid and infectious distempers Let them

them be reported to, and born on the list of patients admitted into, the General Hospital, but remain with the Regimental Surgeons, under their care: Then their rations will be stopped, discounted with the Commissary-General, and in lieu thereof, they will receive supplies of such articles, as the General Hospital can furnish them with; of wine, vinegar, molasses, meal, &c. which I believe would not far exceed the amount of those rations: This would answer to a plan I proposed to your Excellency last winter, and which was approved: Your Excellency only wished then, that some method might be taken to prevent the rations of the sick being twice drawn. I apprehend that matter is fully guarded against, by the method pointed out by the 6th resolve of Congress, of July 17, on the subject of the G. Hospital. The first method would give the greatest satisfaction, not only to the Regimental Surgeons, but to the officers, and to the men; and an experiment would be made of the real expence attending Regimental Hospitals, and every cause, or even shadow of complaint, vanish: It would encourage the soldier in his duty, and if it is found, on trial, subject to any abuse, I imagine that abuse could be easily remedied, by future regulations, or a stoppage in the men's pay, at the time of a new enlistment.

The present increase of the sick is a serious matter, and requires a speedy remedy. I regret the calling for your Excellency's attention (for ever so short a time) to my department; but, I flatter myself, the importance of the subject, and the advantages which may accrue to the service from it, will evince the necessity, and be a sufficient apology for it.

I remain,
Your Excellency's most obedient,
and very humble Servant,
JOHN MORGAN.

ANY man of the least knowledge of the world, that reflects ever so little, will readily own, how disagreeable a piece of business it must be, for any gentleman, to break in upon a Commander in Chief, circumstanced as General WASHINGTON was, with so great a burden of managing an army of undisciplined men, in which the nature and extent of the various departments were so unsettled, and so few officers knew their duty, and therefore teized with numberless applications, which must make him, at times, unavoidably, more difficult of access; and to importune him repeatedly on business, which is supposed to be already settled, either by his own orders, or those of Congress, must be very irksome.

After reading the foregoing letter, can there be a person found, who will not allow that I exerted myself to the very utmost in favour of the Regimental Surgeons, to serve them to the extent of my ability; and after those repeated exertions, and steady perseverance at all times, to promote their reasonable wishes, as far as was consistent with my duty, even in opposition to the sentiments of the General and Congress, when theirs did not agree with my own sentiments; was not the ingratitude and wickedness of those Regimental Surgeons of the deepest dye; because I would not sacrifice to their importunate craving, the duty of my station, and the trust reposed in me, as well as the commands of my superiors; to be guilty, as they were, of private cabals and secret conspiracies, (of which I have lately received full proof,) to injure my character, and misrepresent my conduct, with a view, if possible, to ruin me, for ever, in the public esteem?

THAT none may imagine I wished to reduce the Regimental Surgeons to any improper dependence on myself, which might be assigned as a reason for their opposition to me, I think fit to declare, that I never

sought

sought for any authority over them, inconsistent with their true interest, or upon any occasion, that I was not compelled to assume. On the contrary, I declined those occasions that frequently offered, of making them more dependent upon me, than I knew would be agreeable to themselves, ever since they had taken exceptions to the General's public order at Cambridge, that no Regimental Surgeons should receive commissions in the army to be raised, for the time to come, till they had submitted to such examination of their abilities, as I thought necessary; and had found means to evade it, by prevailing with their Colonels, who (I have been informed) had blank commissions by them, to fill them up with the names of the former Surgeons, without any regard to that order. Yet if I had ever made any representation of this matter to the General, I am convinced, he would not have suffered his own orders to have been dispensed with, in so extraordinary a manner. So far was he from desiring to enlarge their powers, or to lessen my authority, that he was pleased to propose it to me, himself, in one of the last conferences, I had with him, on the subject of regulating the Regimental Surgeons, in order to make them more absolutely dependent upon me, that they should receive warrants at my hands only, for acting in that station. This proposal I declined, on purpose to avoid the envy that would attend so much power, and the consequent misconstructions that, I was confident, would be passed on the most perfect and upright use, that any man, in my post, could make of it. I was desirous to avoid giving room for jealousies to a set of men, of such turbulent and refractory tempers, as I discovered some of them to be, and of which I experienced the ill effects in the instances I have already, and am further to relate, of Mr. Story.

He once called upon me, on business of Colonel Little's Regiment, soon after my arrival from Cambridge to New-York, when I had not yet laid afide all thoughts of finifhing the tafk began at Cambridge, on the genera's order, to examine the Regimental Surgeons, with a view to confirm thofe who were qualified for the office, and to report fuch as were deficient in education, or abilities. He had been previoufly reprefented to me, as a mere firebrand; and as one that was not thought to be properly qualified for a Surgeon's place; whether juftly, or not, I fhall not prefume to fay, as I never proceeded to any examination of his abilities. I afked him whether he acted as Surgeon to that Regiment: He told me that he did. On reminding him of the General's order, for examining the Regimental Surgeons, he behaved in a very infolent, and impertinent manner, giving me to know, "that he had his commiffion already no thanks to me, which was as valid, and of as good authority as my own, and that, truly, he never would fubmit to any examination of mine."

Had I been difpofed to treat him, as he merited on that occafion, I imagine he would have found that I could eafily have obliged him to it, or to quit the fervice: But peace was my object. This made me pafs over his prefent rudenefs of behaviour; and encouraged him in thofe fubfequent acts of infolence, and difhonourable conduct which, I believe, took their rife from the above caufe; and if he was not always at the bottom, yet he always fhewed himfelf to be one of the moft violent agitators, and fomentors of difturbances, that I have ever met with.

* If I may be allowed to mention, in this place, what I take to be the true caufes of the malevolence of the Regimental Surgeons againft me; they were 1ft, my difallowing them to draw ftores, at pleafure, from the G. Hofpital; 2dly, my having recommended it to the General to require fome proof of the qualifications of thofe men, who were to be entrufted with the lives of the fick and wounded foldiery, for which many of them were confcious of

their

their being found unequal to the task, if they were obliged to submit to the inquiry; and 3dly, it was a received opinion of theirs, that the resolve of Congress, "that the Hospital Surgeons and Mates should take rank of the Regimental Surgeons and Mates," was owing to me.

These were unpardonable sins, which they were determined never to forgive nor forget. From the day these last resolutions of Congress were known, they left no scheme untryed to injure my character, and misrepresent my conduct. Of this I have had the strongest assurances from some gentlemen, who, since my dismission, and not before, have informed me of their having received application from those men to join them in their cabals and conspiracy against me; who were struck with astonishment at the proposal, and from the respect which, they were pleased to say, they entertained for my character and conduct, endeavoured to dissuade them from their wicked purposes, and to convince them that I had shewn, in a very striking manner, my inclination to serve them, in the memorial and proposals I had drawn up for that purpose, and the letters I had written to Congress and the General, in their favour; but being bound to act agreeable to my orders, it was not in my power to swerve from them. It was the hope of having prevailed with them, by these remonstrances, to lay aside their intentions, and their ceasing to importune them further on the subject, that inclined them to make no mention of this affair to me, till they afterwards learned they had, though secretly, put their designs into execution, with a success that amazed them.

The acts they pursued to frustrate the intentions of Congress, and to force me to a compliance with their measures; were first, a neglect of reporting the sick for admission into the General-Hospital; the next was their leaving their proper posts with their respective Regiments, and carrying the sick to a distance from the army, where they suffered much, and ascribed all the ill effects of their misconduct, to my not receding from the re-

solutions

folutions of Congrefs: And again, their infufing jealoufies and groundlefs fufpicions into fuch officers as they could influence by their reprefentations, and attempting, by that means, to miflead the General Officers and Members of Congrefs, to my prejudice. Whatever mifchances happened to the fick from their own perverfenefs, or ignorance, were laid by them at my door, as one fo wedded to his own plan, as not to yield to the united voice of all the Regimental Surgeons, to come into their meafures. And, true it is, my perfeverance in what I conceived to be my duty, and for the good of the fervice, was unfhaken; nor could any confideration induce me to deviate from the commands of my fuperiors; although, had the Congrefs feen fit to alter their refolves, in fome particulars, I fhould have thought it would have been for the better, as my letters fully prove.

I am now led, in the order of events, to lay before the public, fome fpecimens of the wickednefs of that fet of men, in counterfeiting, caballing, and endeavouring to make impreffions upon General Officers and others, in their favour, and to my prejudice.

And firft, as to their acts counterfeiting, and paffing what they had counterfeited as a refolve of Congrefs.

Having already mentioned the chagrin and bitternefs of fpirit, which many of them difcovered, on knowing the refolves of Congrefs, July 17; which cut off all their immediate hopes to effect their favorite fcheme, of having Regimental Hofpitals allowed them, on fuch a footing, as to enable them to accumulate ftores at pleafure, and to give them fome difpofal of public monies; it is to be remarked, that what compleated their chagrin was, the determination of Congrefs, which had before raifed the pay of themfelves and Mates, to increafe that of the Hofpital Surgeons and Mates, which was always more than theirs, in fuch proportion as they thought proper; but what above all things kindled their malice and refentment was, that the Congrefs, in

the

the fame vote, had alfo refolved, that the Hofpital Surgeons and Mates fhould take rank of Regimental Surgeons and Mates, as beforementioned, fee page 29.

Let it be remembered, than, to the perpetual infamy of the mean fcandalous fet who were guilty of it, that upon my furnifhing them with a copy of thofe refolves, for the information of all the Surgeons in the army, they made an alteration in the copy of the eighth refolve, by leaving out the particle *of*, and fubftituting the word *with* in its place, which made an entire change of the meaning of that refolve, into another of an oppofite fignification thus foifting in a brat of their own begetting, to ufurp the authority of a vote of Congrefs, they difcovered what their fecret machinations tended to continually, as if this filly device could ferve the purpofe of their wifhes, to lower the eftimation of the General-Hofpital, and raife themfelves into imaginary confequence.

After paffing this counterfeit refolve, and circulating it brifkly, two of their champions, the famous Doctor Story, and an affociate of his, with a view to infult the gentlemen of the Hofpital, went about, exulting in imaginary triumph, to vent their reproachful language againft them, and thereby had nearly accomplifhed what they were intent upon ; which was, to make their fituation fo difagreeable, notwithftanding they never interfered with them, as to induce them rather to quit a ftation that was rendered fo irkfome by them, rather than be fubject to fuch infolence of conduct. One of thofe gentlemen was Doctor Warren, (brother to the deceafed General Warren,) a gentleman, who was fo happy, as to gain the efteem of all who knew him, by his underftanding, his humanity, his affable and polite behaviour, and his great affiduity and attention to difcharge the duties of his ftation : He was at that time acting in the place of a Director of the Military Hofpitals at Long-Ifland, (where, among others, Colonel Little's Regiment was pofted,) with the

title

title and pay only of Surgeon in the General Hofpital, in which he had given great fatisfaction to General Green, and every officer of rank at Long-Ifland, who always fpoke of him, to me, in high terms of approbation. On which, it may not be amifs, tranfiently, to confider this, as a full proof how falutary thofe orders were, which I had given, for providing for the relief and comfortable accommodations of the fick at Long-Ifland, as well as the efficacy with which they were carried into execution, by the wifdom and prudence of the officer who managed the Hofpital department there, by my inftructions.

Difappointed in their malicious defigns, in the firft, they defifted not from other, attempts, to perplex the officers of the General Hofpital; and till their aims were accomplifhed, a party of them determined to leave nothing undone, which they could have hopes of effecting, to produce a prevailing uneafinefs and difcontent in the General Hofpital.

In confequence of my letter to General Wafhington, of July 25th, in favour of the Regimental Surgeons, the Adjutant-General called upon me, by his Excellency's command, to confider how far theirs and my requeft could be granted, confiftently with the intention of Congrefs, without fetting afide their refolves. On which, fuch General Orders were iffued out July 28, as I thought would afford them fome fatisfaction, if the good of the fervice was what they had in view, and not their own private advantage and emolument. But I was greatly miftaken in this fuppofition: They were allowed Regimental Hofpitals under certain reftrictions; amongft which one was, a power given me to fend Hofpital Surgeons to vifit their Hofpitals, to prevent crowding them, and keeping more fick on hand, than they could take good care of, who were to be judges what patients were proper objects for, and directed to receive them into the General Hofpital.

They clamoured exceedingly, drew up an application

cation to the General on that head, which was laid before a Council of General Officers; and some farther points given up to them, by a General order of August the third. The insolence of a party of the Regimental Surgeons rose, in proportion, as they were gratified in any concessions made to them, by the officers of the Hospital, for the sake of peace; who never visited their sick, on that account, but submitted to receive them, as they saw fit to report, and send them to the General Hospital, rather than give room for supposing they had any contention with the Regimental Surgeons: In truth they had not; unless the fire which was kept up, on one side only, by a factious part of the Regimental Surgeons, could be called a contention, and to the keeping up of which, the Hospital Surgeons only contributed by their patience, and suffering for a while, for the good of the service, those men to sport themselves, without interruption, in their unreasonable pursuits, or by opposing them only, with gentle remonstrances. If this is contention, it is of that sort of which Juvenal, in his satyr, gives a lively description, "*ubi tu calcas, ego vapulo tantum.*" or in which one side receives, and the other gives all the blows.

At length, the sense of what was due to themselves wrought so far upon the two eldest of the Hospital Surgeons, Dr. Foster and Dr. Warren, who principally experienced the insolence of those men; that, being unwilling to endure it further, and equally unwilling to be concerned in any disputes with them, they chose rather to quit their present stations: The former let me know his intention to leave the service; and the latter, in a genteel, manly and sensible letter, made known to me his situation, and the resolutions into which this conduct of theirs, had forced him: He represented to me, what he had experienced from the rude and ungovernable temper of this set of men; that, not content with the determination of Congress and the General orders respecting them, they were ever reftlefs, and ever making new and unauthorized demands, inconfiftent with the peace and good government of the General Hofpital; that they were feeking continual occafions for difpute and differences; and as they found the gentlemen of the Hofpital did not chufe, on every occafion, which they knew how to call forth for matter of difputation, to trouble either me or themfelves with frequent references of their difputes, they would gradually gain one point after another, till all their ends were, at laft anfwered, in the fubverfion and ruin of the General Hofpital. In this fituation, as there were daily expectations of the enemys landing at Long-Ifland he flattered himfelf, he could be more ufeful in the military, than in the hofpital department, thus circumftanced; and requefted my permiffion, that he might refign his place in the General Hofpital, and be allowed to act as a volunteer, upon the approaching action.

To have been deprived of the affiftance of thofe gentlemen, at fo critical a time, whofe places I could not have fupplied, with others of equal experience in the conducting of Military Hofpitals, on the plan of the Congrefs, would have thrown the department into that confufion, which a defigning party were bufy to excite, in hopes, by fifhing in troubled waters, to derive thofe advantages to themfelves, in the accomplifhment whereof, their wifhes feemed to center. By explaining to the gentlemen of the Hofpital, the miftake into which this perverfe conduct of the party had led them, and by fupporting their authority, in a proper manner, on every occafion, they were contented to continue in their ftations.

The next meafures thofe men chofe to take, as I have fince learned, from information that I can depend upon, was to intereft fuch officers, over whom they had, or could acquire any influence, to make reprefentations in their behalf, to Members of Congrefs,

and

and to the General. I have cause to believe this was often done to the former, without my having the least intelligence of their proceedings: Of course, I had it not in my power to explain matters, that ought to be known, or to obviate objections, however ill founded. I must, in justice to the General, acknowledge, I have no suspicion that his Excellency ever suffered me to remain long ignorant of any representations, that were made to impeach my conduct by which I was, in all the instances I knew, enabled to answer in my justification to him, and I hope satisfactorily. But I cannot say so of the Congress; for, so far from giving me any information of any such transaction, the Members of whom I have made enquiry, carefully evaded it: Of which I shall have occasion to make more particular mention, in its proper place.

The representations, in favour of Regimental Surgeons, which were calculated to injure me; besides dwelling on the dissatisfaction which the Regimental Surgeons had infused into many of their men, on groundless pretences, and which made some, who knew nothing of the General Hospital themselves, express their dislike against being sent to it; commonly set forth, that it would be highly prejudicial to the service, when a new army was to be raised;—that the sick could not be comfortably accommodated in Regimental Hospitals. The fact is, many of the officers had been chosen, as it were, by the men, who had not a regard to, or any consideration of merit, in that choice, or any love of discipline, but were attached to the persons of the officers they chose, in proportion to the knowledge they had of their being men of the same mean, sordid, grovelling disposition, with many of themselves; void of the sentiments of brave soldiers, love of honour and of liberty on principle, but ready to associate with them on a footing of equality; who would drink drams with them, allow them to plunder, or exempt them from duty, when they did not feel themselves, "*bold to fight*,"

and

and who had no objection to fill the army with maligherers, public extortioners and cowards.

Here a shocking group of disagreeable facts present to my remembrance, in reflecting upon the expedients that have been made use of to raise troops, and the shameful consequences. It is a fact, I believe too generally known to be disputed, that in order to engage men to enter more readily into the service, officers commissions were allowed to men, whose ranks were to be determined by the number of levies they could raise. Prudence, courage, conduct, education, experience, talents, or fitness to command, were not the requisites for officers. No wonder, then, that such kind of men were chosen officers, as many of them were; men of the meanest figure and capacity, such as they termed civil fellows, but in strictness of meaning, Major Sturgeons, or errant Jerry Sneaks, with noses of wax, so very pliant as to be governed by the privates, and many of those, if we may judge of causes by effects, had little in view by entering the service but to make money, by fastening themselves, as leeches, on every thing, from which they could draw pelf. And therefore it was no unusual thing, as I have been often told, when a company was forming, for the men to chuse those, from amongst themselves, for officers, who consented to throw their pay into joint stock with the privates, from which, commissioned and non-commissioned officers; Captains, Lieutenants, Ensigns, Serjeants and Corporals, with drummers and privates, drew equal shares. Some of those, who consented to be privates for one six weeks, three months, or six months, as it happened, expecting to have their turn to command, on a new enlistment, and perhaps to command those very men who were now their officers.

What was to be expected from such men and officers, under no discipline, but to run away, by whole companies, at the appearance of a handful of the enemy. Will any man deny this to be a fact? I will appeal to

one

one instance, out of many. At the approach of an advanced party of the British troops, after the landing at York Island, about three hundred of the men, who were advantageously stationed for opposing them, retreated, without giving fire, with great precipitation; or, in common language, ran-away: They were met by Glover's Regiment, which stopped their flight: As was no unusual thing, on being charged with cowardice, the common men cast the reproach from themselves on their officers, declaring it to be their faults, who, instead of putting themselves at the head of the men, and leading them on to the attack, or there sustaining the charge like soldiers, were the first to scamper off, leaving their company, to fly to such places of safety as they could. The officers of Colonel Glover's regiment, one of the best corps's in the service, and who were indeed gentlemen, immediately obliged the fugitive officers and soldiers, equally, to turn into the ranks with the soldiers of Glover's regiment, and obliged the trembling wretches, to march back to the ground they had quitted. I have been an eye-witness, myself, to whole battalions running off from Powle's-Hook, and the heights of Bergen, upon the firing of a broad side from a man of war, in her failing down the North River to join the fleet below, when obliged to remove from her station, to avoid a fire-ship, although not a man was hurt by that fire. These doughty champions never stopped till they came to Second River, but forced away the very waggons that were impressed to transport the sick, and those wounded at Long-Island, to Newark; to carry off themselves and baggage, for many of them chose to ride, to save their legs, in case of being more nearly pursued. A cannon being planted in the causeway, that commanded the ferry at Second River, was pointed towards them, by an officer of artillery, who commanded there; and who threatened to mow them down, if they did not return to their posts. What was their next shift? They betook themselves to a ferry a mile above:

above: The boats happened to be on the other side, but within reach of their shot; on which, being fearful of any delay, they called out to the ferrymen to hasten over with their boats, or they would discharge a volley upon them; and thus, they made good their retreat!

When such were the officers, is it to be wondered at, or rather is it to be believed? But how incredible soever it may appear to those at a distance it is an indisputable truth that a Captain was tried and broke, by a Court-Martial, for stealing his soldiers blankets, the minutes of which Court-Martial are not only published amongst ourselves, but reprinted in the New-York or Newport papers; and one officer, in the face of the General's family, and many officers of distinction, was found shaving his men, acting in so menial a capacity, long after the retreats from Long-Island and New-York, whether for the pence he could collect, or that he might stand a chance of interest and preferment, and *"that he might not be prejudicial to the service when a new army was to be raised,"* let casuists determine. Whether giving ear to the unreasonable clamours of such men as these, and the gratifying them, by indulgences in their senseless demands, dismissing an officer of distinguished rank and trust, for non-compliance with them, against the express commands of Congress, was the most likely means of promoting the service, or procuring respect and veneration for the Congress itself, time will manifest, *credat Judæus, non ego.*

What instances of thieving, plundering and oppression, both in officers and men, have come to my knowledge, that would disgrace the lawless Arab, the barbarous Scythian, the rude Goth, or wild and savage Tartar; who spare their own, when they war on their enemies!

"Birds prey on birds, fish on each other prey,
"But man alone, does kindred man betray."

I

I was present when a lady from West-Chester, lodged a complaint with a General Officer, against a Captain of the regiment of artificers, who had got into her house, and under pretence of protecting her, as a friend, from the incursions of the enemy, robbed her of a trunk, containing many costly articles; silks and other wearing apparel, to the amount of fourteen hundred pounds; and disposed of her cloaths at a public sale, which being proved upon him, he was justly cashiered.

From my own knowledge, and indeed my particular loss, having been a great sufferer, I can declare that what the enemy have spared to our own people, less compassionate men, from amongst ourselves, have carried off and destroyed; and Hessian cruelty to an enemy, has been exceeded by the more savage cruelty of the very men, paid by us, to defend our property. An injured man has a right to complain; and truth will force conviction on the minds of fellow-men, however harsh and ungrateful it may be, to some, to hear the truth.

But that I may not pass beyond the limits of my own department, and what has a connexion with it, I will confine myself in the instances I shall now exhibit of disorderly conduct to those facts, of which I came to the knowledge, in the discharge of my duty, and the opposition I met with in the discharge thereof. I pass over other examples of oppressing helpless women, and families of the best fortune and distinction, on whom sick and well, indiscriminately, have been forced, or men that ought to have been reported to the General Hospital, for my Directions; which no regard has been had, whether the persons were well disposed, or otherwise affected, to the cause of American Freedom; but " *tros rutilusve fuat, nullum discrimen habetor*," The object was to get possession of their houses and property, under the pretext of accommodating the soldiery, and particularly for Regimental Hospitals. I

shall

shall select one case, in which were complicated, disregard to Congress, disrespect and breach of the General's orders, opposition to the General Hospital, which sustained great injury from such proceedings, and great inhumanity to the fair and weak part of the creation. The circumstances of which are well known to some, who are officers of rank in the army, and of irreproachable honour, to whom, if necessary, I can appeal, in support of what I advance.

About the month of August, 1776, having made frequent representations at Head-Quarters, that I could not obtain regular reports from the Regimental Surgeons, of the state of their sick; but that they were seizing on those very houses for regimental sick, that were assigned to me, by the State of New-York, for the use of the General Hospital; an order was issued, requiring the Regimental Surgeons to deliver in the reports I had demanded, &c. and to inforce it, all Colonels, and Commanders of Regiments were called upon, to make it known to their Surgeons, that they might not plead ignorance, and were directed to see that the order was duly observed.

Just at that time, a Brigade newly arrived from the Massachusetts-Bay Government, under command of General Fellows, was ordered to be stationed along the river, from Greenwich to Chelsea and upwards, to throw up lines, and defend the same against any attempts of the enemy to land there. Most of the houses fit for the accommodation of the officers of that Brigade, and, for quartering of the men, being previously seized upon by the Regimental Surgeons, for themselves and their sick; Colonel Moylan, then Quarter-master General, desired we might ride out together, to take a view of the sick, and of the houses in that quarter. He ordered a large dwelling house, on the estate of the deceased Admiral Warren, then in possession of certain Regimental sick, to be evacuated, and cleansed for the accommodation of the officers of the Brigade, posted in the

the neighbourhood, to whom therefore it was very convenient, as it adjoined the works thrown up for defence of the landing, but a very improper place to contain sick persons, as it was close to the bank of the river, and particularly exposed to the firing of the ships, that might pass up or down the same.

The very mention of dispossessing the Regimental Surgeons of their Hospital, gave great dissatisfaction, though I undertook to receive their sick into the General Hospital. That proposal met with opposition. That the Surgeon might have a place for the accommodation of his patients, I informed him of a large commodious barn of Mr. Campbell's at Greenwich, with two spare rooms on the back part, and lower floor of the house, at a small distance, adjoining the kitchen, being rooms the best sheltered from the shot of passing men of war, and most retired from the river. Such spacious, airey barns as the above, well floored, and secure from rain, yet cool, and pervious to the wind, answer to the places, recommended by Sir John Pringle physician to the British army, in a former war, as proper for hospitals. Such, assuredly, are better calculated for the recovery of dysenteric and putrid diseases, that prevailed at this time, to any of the dwelling houses, with plaistered walls, and small or confined chambers, which, though convenient for a private family, are not proper for the crowding of sick into them. But fine houses were commonly preferred by the Regimental Surgeons; and this gentleman let me know, that he should expect to be broke, if he consented to accept of a barn, however commodious, for the reception of his sick.

The house itself, he could not have, it being pre-occupied by another Surgeon, for the use of a Regimental Hospital. On looking into the rooms, they were found to be filled with the sick, and the Surgeon who had the care, panting for breath, in the midst of them, It was amidst the sultry heats of summer: In vain I represented to him the danger of engendring a putrid malignant fever, from crowding so many sick, in confined rooms, in that hot season He had near a hundred sick in the house: I forbad him then, as I had uniformly prohibited every Regimental Surgeon I conversed with on the subject, from taking charge of more than thirty or forty sick, on the outside, at any one time, being a larger number than they could well attend; as I desired to know how they intended to manage, if called to the field of battle, or on any sudden removal of their regiments, an event daily expected, and they encumbered with so many sick. As the other Surgeon had refused to occupy the barn, and shady rooms on the ground floor, back of the house, I recommended it to him, to send at least one half of his sick to the General Hospital, and remove the greater part of the men into the barn: He disregarded my advice, a putrid fever prevailed, he caught the infection, and paid the forfeiture of his rashness, with his life.

I then went to General Heath, who commanded that division of the army, and represented the matter to him; and as it was but a small distance from his quarters, requested him to give himself the trouble, of seeing with his own eyes, and judging himself of the truth of the facts I related. The General, in polite terms, declined my most importunate solicitation, upon this unanswerable objection, that it might look, as if he made himself a party against the Regimental Surgeons.

As the Surgeon had never made his report, and the order had been issued a week, I had waited on the Lieutenant-Colonel of the regiment, in person, before I saw the Surgeon, and complained of his neglect, in not reporting his sick, and in not sending such as exceeded the number he could take care of, to the General Hospital. I reminded him that, by the General Order, he was required to see that the Surgeon complyed with said order. The answer he gave me, was in these very words: "That the Regimental Surgeons could read the orders for themselves; and if not, he should give himself

self no trouble about it ; adding, that, if it was in his power to prevent it, none of his men should ever be carried to a General Hospital."

Perhaps it may be imagined from such a reply, he had reason to assert, that the General Hospital was not kept in a clean and proper state, and that the Regimental Hospitals were: The reverse of which was true: The former were always kept clean and airey, and, in the words of General Green's letter, which I shall have occasion to publish at large, " *well provided with every thing, and the sick very comfortable ;*" whereas most of the Regimental Hospitals, I had ever seen, on account of the filth and nastiness of them, deserved the appellation they have acquired in the Eastern Governments, of pest-houses ; for such they commonly turned out to be. I asked him his reasons: He made no reply to my question ; but required of me to give him an order, which it seems he thought proper to demand of me, in favour of his Surgeon, for a number of bed frames.

This led me to shew in what manner the Regimental Surgeons, and such officers, were ever at work, by their plans, and method of proceeding to exhaust, unfurnish, or prevent the supplies of the General Hospital, all in their power. I had engaged the Quartermaster General, to give orders in his department, for making a large number of bed frames, for the sick of the General Hospital. So fast as forty or fifty were made, the Regimental Surgeons, with, or without orders from their officers, applyed for, and carried them away. Colonel Moylan, told the Officer in my hearing, " that they had carried off above two thousand, that were intended for the General Hospital; which of course, could not be provided with them as fast as was wanted." Upon every movement of a regiment, that required a shifting of the houses for Regimental Hospitals, many of the bed frames were left behind, or burned, or carried off ; and the Surgeons, probably,

probably, made fresh applications for others, whilst the General Hospital could not be provided with spare bedsteads, for additional sick, or wounded that might be sent in.

On that occasion, I remonstrated in favour of the General Hospital, and had a stop put to the further supplies of bed frames to the Regimental Surgeons, till that was better furnished. Upon this, and in like instances, I have been visited by some of the militia Colonels and Brigadiers who, by their representations, seemed to think it a hard case, that I would not concur with their Surgeons and them, to subvert the General Hospital, which I was appointed to establish and govern; to enable them, contrary to the designs of Congress, the General's Orders, and the very nature of things, to transfer all the property and power of the General Hospital, to Regimental Surgeons. Colonel Moylan then and often, told me, that by the repeated concessions I was making to those men, he should not wonder if they succeeded, in what he saw they were aiming at, to subvert the General Hospital, and plant themselves on the ruins, to the confusion of all order and discipline.

But to return from this relation, which being connected with, and part of the subject I am upon, is not an improper digression, I now resume the narrative of that particular instance of brutal conduct, which I have had in view, to illustrate my declaration of encroaching on my department, by an outrage upon all military order and discipline, and on humanity itself.

Mr. Campbell, who had purchased a lease of the house aforementioned, at Greenwich, from Mr Delancey, was a stranger, and with his lady and family of children, of whom he had several, all young, and some mere infants, came into America to settle, about the time our unhappy disputes, with Great Britain, began, or soon after they began to be attended with such consequences, as civil war and bloodshed. Congress

being

being satisfied that he had not come over to America, with any inimical intention of taking part in the dispute, against this country, saw fit, as I am informed, to grant him their protection; on the faith of which he determined to become an American, by settling here with his family: He chose the neighbourhood of New-York, for his residence, and leased the house, with the estate, already mentioned, at Greenwich, where he conducted himself inoffensively and irreproachably. The lustful eye of some of the Regimental Officers, or Surgeons, marked it out for a Regimental Hospital. I had the account from Mr. Campbell's own mouth, with circumstances that gained my credit to his relation: He informed me, that without any previous notice to depart, and resting on the assurances of the Quartermaster General, that he should not displace him, (for he saw no occasion for it;) a gallant officer came up one day to the house, followed with a long train of sickly soldiers, who were ill, with dysenterys, putrid, and other fevers, and put them in possession of his house, without any regard to the owner, or to the circumstances of his family, as if on purpose to drive them out from their habitation.

This he effected; but not immediately, as Mr. Campbell had no other house in which he had a right, or that he could hope for liberty, to shelter himself, his wife and helpless children; nor before these, who were of a delicate frame were seized with the infection, and nearly destroyed by the filth of the sick, which had drove them from room to room, till they had no farther retreat. On attempting mildly to expostulate with the officer and to know, if he acted by any authority, or command of the Quartermaster General or other superior officers, this heroic man, just deigned, with a magisterial air, to spend as much precious breath, as to acquaint him, he wanted not to exchange conversation, or to throw words away, unnecessarily, upon him; and triumphantly turning on his heel, faced to the right about;

about; and left him astonished at so unfeeling and barbarous an insult. Beset in this manner, with objects of terror, and disgust, which were hourly increasing, he hastened with his family, from their own house, to seek cover elsewhere: The most of the family, to my own knowledge, as I had occasion to meet with them in one of the houses in the neighbourhood, assigned to me for an hospital, for they applied to me for relief, very narrowly escaped, if they did all escape, perishing, in consequence of the putrid dysentery, contracted as above.

It is, with great aversion, at the recollection of this distressing scene, that I but faintly delineate it, not without throwing a veil over such parts, as shock me, accustomed, as I have ever been, to hospitals and sick, when I connect the ideas of delicacy in breeding and manners, and what protection is due to female dignity and helpless infancy, with such more than savage treatment, not of enemies, but of friends and strangers! *Quis talia fando temperat a lachrymis!*

As I cannot prevail on myself to dwell longer on scenes, whereof this is but one of many that have offered to my notice, and not less distressing, I hasten, from them, to try if I can recover some less offensive grounds, on which to proceed. A man that can enter into minute descriptions of particulars, so disgustful and distressing, may seem to have lost his finer feelings; but if any man can have any gratification in wading through the dirty puddles of such business, he must have a strange perverseness of taste indeed: Are there men that would take delight in painting a Demon, in all the shocking picture of black deformity? Let them do it, I cannot; but being compelled in my vindication I have touched the subject slightly. The many things that have intruded upon my memory, on this occasion, I have endeavoured to refuse admittance, wishing to bury the whole in oblivion, to rise no more in judgment against us.

Of

Of the Regimental Surgeons and Mates, I will only observe this once, that as I have done justice to those of them, who merited it, by declaring there were some amongst them of liberal manners, education and abilities ; ,I must be permitted to declare, there were many, very many of them, unlettered, ignorant, and rude to a degree scarcely to be imagined. Some of them, I have been informed, and from what I observed, could readily believe, were never educated to the profession of physick, nor had ever seen an operation of Surgery : Many of them had but small appearances of either literature or breeding, in which respect they fell short of some of the privates. It would display a farce of the most ridiculous kind, to give the public an account of the learning and attainments, which some of them, whom I have had an opportunity of examining, have discovered; or to give a transcript of their reports. And that this ignorance was pretty general, may be safely inferred from their repugnance to stand the test of inquiry, so contrary to the practice of those, who are men of talents, improved by education, who shun no occasion, of giving proof thereof, by their compliance with those laws and regulations, which the wisdom of States or the good policy of seminaries, and corporations of the learned in the profession, devise, to encourage genius and merit, and to put a stop to the rapid growth of empyricism : And I observed, that it was generally the most ignorant, the most opiniated and the most disorderly, and irregular in their conduct, who were the most troublesome, and loudest in their clamours. These were the men, from whom I found the greatest opposition, to every regulation for introducing method, discipline and improvement, into the department of physick and surgery.

It is with much regret I have yielded to the necessity I have been under, in clearing up my own conduct from the imputations of a set of wicked men, to display the true character and behaviour of those, who
were

were my accufers, and from the many famples of ra-pine, diforder and oppreffion of which they have been guilty, to felect fome of their nefarious practices, and of fuch amazing prodigality, as, if it were allowed to pafs without notice, would have been fufficient to infure deftruction to any army, or people. I am fully perfwaded that we owe many of the misfortunes and mifcarriages of laft campaign, to thofe men, who were guilty of them. I have but barely fkimmed over the furface of them. A reluctance to enter deeper into fuch a fink has reftrained me: Were I to attempt an enumeration of them all, time would fail.

It is fufficient to fhew their deftructive tendency, in general; to make a remark on the mean and fordid practice, which was purfued by fome of the Regimental Surgeons, of felling certificates for furloughs and difcharges, at a lefs fum than a fhilling a man. At this rate, a number equal to a regiment might be difcharged for a much lefs fum, than has been fince given, to raife a fingle recruit. At a moderate computation, fo many men have been born on fome fick lifts of Regimental Surgeons, including waiters, fit for duty, that if the practice was common, the ftrongeft Brigade in the army was not equal to the number thus maintained in idlenefs. I am willing to hope that thofe inftances of mal-practice I have adduced are fufficient to fhut the door againft the like abufes in future, and to introduce better difcipline, and better men into ftations of public truft: And that men of better principle, as well as of more knowledge and humanity, are engaged in the prefent fervice. To promote the interefts of thefe, were the motives of my conduct, and the object I invariably purfued in all my propofed regulations.

Amongft thofe in employ the laft year, fome, in the time of need, deferted the army altogether, and others fhunned to attend their regiments to the field of battle.

It was a general complaint, that at the battle of the

the White-Plains, few of the Regimental Surgeons were with their respective Battalions, in consequence of which, many of the wounded bled to death, who, it was supposed, might have been saved, had they been present, and done their duty: Their absence obliged me to fix myself at the lines, with some of the Hospital Surgeons. This produced the following circular letter to be sent round the country, with orders to the Surgeons of the General Hospital who were at a distance from camp, to call upon the Regimental Surgeons, in pursuance of the resolves of Congress, and the General's commands, to deliver up all their sick to the Hospital, and to return to their proper posts, signed, with the following declaration.

"I have read, and much approve of those instructions and orders."

G. WASHINGTON.

CIRCULAR LETTER.

To the Regimental Surgeons and Mates, belonging to the Army of his Excellency General WASHINGTON, now absent, with, or without the sick of their respective Regiments and Brigades; on either side of Hudson's River.

GENTLEMEN,

FEW of the Surgeons or sick, allowed to remove from camp, some time ago, being yet returned, and no report made of them to me, His Excellency the Commander in Chief, conceives, that his former indulgence to the sick, in permitting them to retire from camp, for the recovery of their health, has been much abused, both by the sick, and the generality of the Surgeons and Mates, under whose care they were allowed that indulgence: It is his Excellency's orders, therefore, that each of you do forthwith wait upon Isaac Foster, Esq; at Newark, John Warren, Esq; at Hackinsack, or Philip Turner, Esq; at Norwalk; Surgeons in the General Hospital, whoever of them is nearest at hand, and make a faithful and accurate report of the state of the sick and wounded under your care, and remove those who are fit subjects, immediately, to the General Hospital, under their care; for which you are to apply to the Quartermaster General's department, for waggons, and accompany them yourselves. Such of you as those gentlemen require to assist them for the present, in the General Hospital, and who are willing to attend their sick there, under their direction, are allowed to do so, till further orders; all others are to repair immediately to Head-Quarters, and join their respective regiments; first furnishing me with an accurate register, duly certified, of the state of the sick that went out with them, or have been since under their care, specifying the time of their being taken ill, their diseases, and events as to death, recovery or continuance; and whether any of the sick have been allowed to withdraw from under their care, and when. As all, who are absent without leave, must naturally be looked upon as deserters. And the Surgeons or Mates, who cannot give a regular and satisfactory account of the faithful discharge of their duty, necessarily subject themselves to an inquiry into their conduct.

JOHN MORGAN, Director-General and Physician in Chief.

Camp at the White-Plains, *November* 5, 1776.

AMONGST other methods used by the Regimental Surgeons, to accomplish their purposes, I have mentioned their infusing jealousies and groundless suspicions into such officers as they could influence by their representations, fentations, in hopes, by their means, to miflead the General Officers, and Members of Congrefs, to my prejudice.

I do not pretend to have knowledge of all the applications that have been made, to different Members of Congrefs, to give weight to the clamours of the Regimental Surgeons; but one of them, that I do not know of, requires my ferious attention.

Having called one day, upon General Green, to confult him about fome regulations of the hofpitals, I found him bufy in writing a letter to the Prefident of Congrefs, complaining much of the fufferings of the fick, for want of fuch eftablifhment, as provided properly for taking good care of them. Not the leaft notice was taken of the unwearied pains I had beftowed to accomplifh that purpofe; which might lead Congrefs to imagine me very negligent of my duty, or inattentive to matters that fo nearly concerned me: I to him fo: He then added a poftfcript, in which he fee... d barely to guard againft reflexions upon me; yet ... ore to do me that juftice, which I thought myfelf ... ntitled to expect from him, if to be had from ... in the army.

I l... General Green in two dangerous fits of ill ... ch he had proofs of my attention to him, ... duity to the bufinefs of my ftation, that men ... far different return. The laft was at a time, when Gen... l Green had the command at Long-Ifland, and about the time when the enemy were landed not many miles below. Although I was then inceffantly engaged on New-York Ifland, I made all other bufinefs give way to my daily attendance on him; and finding his life endangered, by a putrid and billious fever, under which he laboured, prevailed with him to leave the ifland, and provided him with one of the moft healthy, airey, fafeft and beft accommodated habitations, in the center, betwixt the two rivers, two miles diftant from the city of New-York. My place of duty changed, likewife,

and

and my presence was demanded every day at Long-Island, to attend to the care and removal of the wounded. Yet I visited him, daily, once, twice or oftner, under a variety of difficulties, and watched over him with the strictest attention, and an affection little less than fraternal, till his recovery was so far compleated, [that he] was out of all danger. I should not have given [an] account of matters, but for the following reason, [which] is, because it was at General Green's [request I erected] a General Hospital at Long-Island, [for that] part of the army under his command, [and so w]ell conducted by Doctor Warren, [that is needless] to pass high encomiums on its [merit. The Counc]il of General Officers, held [and subscribed] by the Regimental Surgeons, [was grou]ndless and unreasonable. [If there was any d]eficiency in either that part of the [general hos]pital itself, or any want in the accommo[dation of] the sick of the regiments stationed there, [which coul]d be obtained, the fault must be laid at his [door,] and his only, because he had expressly engaged, [on] my first consenting, in compliance with his request, to provide a General Hospital there; to build or furnish sufficient quarters for all the sick belonging to that division of the army under his command; and because by my orders to Doctor Warren, my instructions to the Regimental Surgeons, July 3d, and General Washington's order, matters were so regulated that the sick might remain under the care of their own Surgeons, in such quarters or hospitals as General Green himself might order for them; and be considered as parts of one General Hospital, of which Doctor Warren was to be esteemed the Director and Head: They were to be allowed all necessary refreshments, and the Regimental Surgeons and their sick might partake of every advantage, which the sick in the General Hospital enjoyed, under the immediate care of the Hospital Surgeons, if the Regimental Surgeons would consider themselves as

acting

acting under the direction of the General Hospital, with this only restriction, that every demand was to be made, and granted under the acknowledged authority of Doctor Warren, to whom I had entrusted all my own power for their good, for which he was to be accountable: And I forbad him to deliver out any stores, of any kind, to the Regimental Surgeons, for the sick, not reported to, and considered as in the General Hospital.

A second reason, is the following letter from General Green to General Washington, of August 11th.

A third reason, is my having been censured, for delaying to communicate to the Congress the plan of regulations I had promised to draw up for their consideration, so long after I had undertaken it, during all which time it was left with Gen. Green, for the benefit of his observations and remarks, viz. from about the middle or end of October to the 20th of December, although I repeatedly applied to him by message and letter, to expedite it for that purpose; and it was then returned to me in the state I delivered it, without any remark to accompany it.

And lastly, the liberty which Doctor Story took, of making use of General Green's name, to sanctify his assertions, that the sufferings of the sick lay at my door.

On these several accounts, I now call on General Green (in a more especial manner) and on any, and every other officer, of whatever rank, whether General or Field Officers, or those of inferior rank, who have thought fit to make any representations, either to Congress as a body, or to particular Members of it, or to the Commander in Chief, concerning the causes of the sufferings of the sick, if they can lay any thing to my charge, whether relating to the disposal of Hospital Stores, the disposition of public monies, or any other article entrusted to me: I desire to know if they can accuse me of any neglect of duty, of indolence,

lence, inactivity, inattention to the calls of my station, or of any breach, either of General Orders, or of the Resolves of Congress: If they can do any of these, I shall be glad they will publish it to the world, in a manner that will afford me an opportunity to reply, in print. Did ever any General, Field Officer, or other, on any suggestion of the sick suffering for want of care, visit the General Hospital, and judging with his own eyes, report to me a single instance of the sort? I declare they never did: So that the complaints of the sufferings of the sick, are not of those under my care, but of those that were hindered from coming, or who were never reported to the General Hospital, for admission. On the contrary, the complaints ever were, that *"whilst in the General Hospital, the sick were well taken care of, they could not enjoy the like advantages in Regimental Hospitals,"* But if so, the fault of not sending them to the General Hospital, is the more conspicuous, and the wickedness of ascribing the sufferings of the sick to the General Hospital, or myself, from whose care they were kept back, and which is justly chargeable on the Regimental Surgeons, who kept them back, and the officers who supported them in such a contumacious disobedience of every order, of the Congress and General, is the more flagrant. But, let us attend to General Green's letter.

GENERAL GREEN's LETTER

TO HIS EXCELLENCY

GENERAL WASHINGTON,

Camp at Long-Island, *Aug.* 11, 1776.

DEAR GENERAL,

THERE is no proper establishment for supplying the Regimental Hospitals with proper utensils for the sick; they suffer therefore for want of proper accommodation.

commodation. There is repeated complaints on that head. The Regimental Hospitals are, and ever will be rendered useless, nay grievous, unless there is some proper fund, to provide the necessary conveniences. The General Hospital cannot receive all the sick; and those that are in the Regimental Hospitals, are in a suffering condition. If this evil continues, it must greatly injure the service, as it will dispirit the well, to see the sick suffer, and prevent their engaging again, upon any conditions whatever. Great humanity should be exercised, towards those indisposed. Kindness upon one hand, leaves a favorable and lasting impression, neglect and suffering on the other, is never forgotten.

I am sensible, there has formerly been great abuses in the Regimental Hospitals, but I am in hopes, men of better principles are elected to those places, and that the same evils will not happen again. But the Continent had better suffer a little extraordinary expence, than the sick should be left to suffer, for want of those conveniences that may be easily provided.

I would beg leave to propose, that the Colonels of regiments be allowed to draw monies, to provide the Regimental Hospitals, with proper utensils; an account of the disbursements weekly, or monthly, to be rendered: This will prevent abuse, and remedy the evil.

Something is necessary to be done, speedily, as many sick are in a suffering condition.

The General Hospital is well provided with every thing, and the sick very comfortable. I wish it was extensive enough to receive the whole, but it is not.

I am, your Excellency's most obedient Servant,

NATH. GREEN.

I SHALL now take the liberty of propounding a few questions, on the contents of the above letter.

WAS General Green acquainted with the resolves of
Congress,

Congress, of July 17, page 29? If so, has not his letter a direct tendency to oppose and overset them?

What reason can be assigned for Regimental Hospitals being established on Long-Island, with all the furniture and apparatus of a General Hospital, when the sick might have the benefit of the General Hospital there, in compliance with General Green's own request, although a very improper place for establishing an Hospital, where the enemy were expected to land, especially when there was a General Hospital on the Island of New-York, for the reception of those who could not be accommodated at Long-Island?

Of what use could Regimental Hospitals be at Long-Island; or rather, with what disservice must they be attended, when the enemy were expected to land there? Was it to retain more sick there, to embarrass the army, when the works were besieged, or to keep Regimental Soldiers from accompanying their corps into the field, in case it was judged expedient to march forth, to meet the enemy at a distance, from the lines; or was it convenient, at such times, to be discharging many hundreds of sick, in the time of action, upon the Hospital Surgeons on the Island, at the same time with the wounded?

It is said the General Hospital cannot receive all the sick, and those in the Regimental Hospitals were in a suffering condition. Had any been reported to the General Hospital at Long-Island, that were ever refused admission? I never heard of an instance. But if there was no room at Long-Island, was there no room in the General Hospital at New-York? Would neither the College, with all its spacious apartments; the City Hospital, with all its great and magnificent conveniences; the City Barracks, capable of accommodating above a thousand men; the many vacant houses in the Bowry, or neighbourhood of New-York, and whole streets, appropriated for the purpose, and assigned to the Director-General, by the Convention of the State of New-York, and the City Committee, and to be at his difpofal only: I fay, were not all thefe fufficient for their reception and accommodation? If not, he had the choice of moſt of the country feats, for the fpace of feven miles from the city, to anfwer that purpofe. And were not thefe enough?

But fuppofe it to have been neceffary for the fick to be accommodated on Long-Ifland: What reafon can be affigned, if they were to be permitted to draw ftores and furniture from the General Hofpital, why they fhould not range themfelves under the direction of Doctor Warren, which was the only poffible method, that, with much reflexion, could be devifed to entitle them to the neceffaries and comforts, which it was allowed the General Hofpital was well provided with? Could the Regimental Surgeons, who were fo earneft for having feparate and diftinct Hofpitals, have any thing in view, by remaining unaccountable for their fupplies? What other reafon could they have for refufing to have the ftate of their fick infpected by Hofpital Surgeons, with a power to order fuch fick, as appeared to be proper objects, into the General Hofpital, but to retain as many fick, or nominal fick, as they pleafed, on their lifts, till the time of an action, and then to pour them all into the General Hofpital, and to receive the wounded under their care, for the fake of trying experiments, and of performing operations, which fome of them had never feen performed? From all their actions, it is plain this was an object they had much at heart. And what would that be, but to reduce Gentlemen, of the firft clafs in their profeffion, to be fubordinate to all their purpofes, and meer minifters of their pleafure?

For what purpofe are fuperior rank and greater pay allowed to Hofpital, than to Regimental Surgeons, if not to engage men of the firft ability, education, and experience, to take that charge upon them?

And after all, is there any thing propofed in General

ral Green's letter, that I had not urged before, both to General Green himself, as well as to General Washington and the Congress, for the relief of the Regimental Surgeons, who might be situated at some distance from the General Hospital ? Wherefore, if there could be any exception made to the plan, it must be to except those on Long-Island, where it was unfit there should be Regimental Hospitals, when the enemy were expected to land there, and when there was a General Hospital at hand, of which they might have the same benefits, with those under the immediate care of the Hospital Surgeons and Mates ; if they would submit to the same regulations.

Upon the whole of this inquiry ; when the Congress who, for ought General Green knew to the contrary, might be supposed to have weighed matters deliberately, had fixt upon a plan, which, by every subsequent set of resolves, restricted the Regimental Surgeons, within narrower limits than before ; or, at least, enforced the former, with new and additional weight : Where was the necessity, expedience, or propriety, of supporting the Regimental Surgeons in their clamours ? They were ever backward to send their sick to the General Hospital, to have a plea for Regimental Hospitals, and to draw stores at discretion, which never was allowed in any army, and which Congress had not seen fit to allow them ? Would it not have been more consistent with the idea of submission to the commands of our superiors, if General Green, instead of giving that weight to the prejudices, and ignorance in point of duty, and in the proper management of the sick of an army, which the Surgeons laboured under, had seen fit to have enjoined their making weekly returns of their sick to the General Hospital, for admission, agreeable to the orders of Congress ; and thereby helped to cure or remove those prejudices ? This might have checked them in their career, of aspersing reputations to accomplish

their

their aims, and must have contributed to their own ease, and the great benefit of the suffering sick.

But whilst Regimental Surgeons were so intent upon the establishment of Hospitals for their regiments, and General Green was so earnest in seconding their desires, by his application to the President of the Congress, and Commander in Chief: What was the opinion of General Washington, if we are to judge by his orders? They agreed with the resolves of Congress: And as to the Members of Congress, all that I ever heard speak of them, exactly corresponded with Mr. Gerry, who wrote me his opinion of the matter, in the following words: " With respect to small Regimental Hospitals, I cannot but think them an unnecessary and dangerous institution; for, upon every removal of such regiments, those Hospitals are a dead weight, and must be removed, or be exposed to the enemy. The latter, you will agree, is by no means admissible; and the removing such Hospitals, is attended with hardships to the diseased, and prevents them from an early recovery."

Let us attend to what he next writes, of REGIMENTAL SURGEONS: " As to the REGIMENTAL SURGEONS, says he, being otherwise wholly USELESS, I have always supposed, that they were never intended to answer any other purpose, in time of war, than to cure, in camp, slight wounds and diseases, by which the patients were not confined, and to attend the regiments, in time of action; to dress the wounded soldiers, until they can be removed to the General Hospital."

Where persons of rank and influence, as General Officers and Members of Congress, draw such different ways, is it possible for any man, to conduct in such a manner, betwixt them, as to give satisfaction to every one?

But that it may be seen, how I endeavoured to discharge my duty, by adhering exactly to my orders, where they restricted me to a point; and yet in prudentials accommodated myself, as well as I could, to the

reasonable

reasonable desires of others: I shall here publish a copy of my directions, to Doctor Warren, for establishing, and for the manner of conducting the Hospitals, under his care, at LONG-ISLAND.

INSTRUCTIONS TO JOHN WARREN, Esquire, SURGEON of the GENERAL HOSPITAL.

S I R, *New-York, June* 12, 1776.

YOU are desired to go over to Long-Island, and to consult with General Green, about the proper houses for the forming of an Hospital (to be part of the General Hospital) for the reception of the sick in his Brigade. For your assistants, you will be pleased to take over three of the Hospital Mates, of which Mr. Glover is to be one, the other two as you agree with the other Surgeons.

Make out a proper assortment of medicines, such a list as you think needful, after consulting with Doctors Foster, Adams and M'Knight, and order it to be put up from the Hospital stores: If you have occasion for further assistants, make a requisition from General Green's Brigade, of as many Surgeons and Mates as you shall stand in need of.

Keep a register of the sick, in which you are to make an entry of the times of their admission and discharge, as well as of the diseases they labour under, and require of the respective Surgeons of the different regiments, weekly returns of the sick in the Hospital belonging to their regiments, in order to compare with yours: From which, once a month, a roll is to be made out for receiving the ration money, from the Commissary General; which you will get signed by the Brigadier-General, after you have compared it with the return of sick born on the rolls of the Regimental Surgeons: From the time they are admitted into the General Hospital,

their

their rations are to be stopped in the regiments: The list of the Regimental Surgeons, compared with yours, ought to be delivered by them to the Adjutant or Quartermaster of every regiment, in order to prevent rations being drawn for the sick, in the regiments, so long as they remain in the hospital.

You will be pleased to fix up, in the hospital, the regulations already agreed upon by the Surgeons of the Hospital, for the government of the officers, nurses, attendants and patients; and appoint some person to have them read in every ward: The rules of diet, ought to be fixed up in the same place, and a strict attention paid to the same.

You are to take over Mr. Weld, to act as a Storekeeper, who is to obey your commands in all things relating to his department: Whatever stores you have occasion for, in the department of the Commissary-General, or Quartermaster-General, you will apply for by an order under your hand, signed by order of the Director-General, with your name, of which direct the Storekeeper to keep an exact account, and of the distribution of the same.

What nurses you require for the sick, you will engage at the price of half a dollar per week; the number not to exceed one for every ten persons, sick or wounded; the necessary labourers to be employed by the day, as usual, in which avoid engaging a greater number than is absolutely necessary.

Deliver out no stores of any kind to the Regimental Surgeons: When the sick require further aids than they can give, let them be reported to you, and if their cases require, receive them into the General Hospital.

Take with you at least 1500 bandages, and a quantity of tow, with a set of capital instruments, and all suitable dressings, in case of an action.

Use your best endeavours to make the Surgeons and Mates of the regiments attentive to their duty.

For any debts contracted for the use of the General-Hospital,

Hospital, agreeable to the above rules, draw on me. You will emp'oy the same person to supply fresh meat, and at the same prices, as in the hospital at New-York.

Weekly returns of the sick to be sent over early every Monday morning as usual.

Be pleased to call on Mr. Delamater, for 100 additional blankets, for the use of the hospital in Long-Island, and as many beds, applying to the Quartermaster for straw, from time to time, and order the nurses, washer women, &c. to clean them from time to time.

An orderly Mate is to take charge of the blankets, and bedding, &c. and of the Hospital furniture every week; to enter into a book for the purpose, what stores of this kind are given out, to examine what each sick brings with them, and to see that nothing is carried out, on their dismission, not belonging to them.

An orderly serjeant, or corporal, or careful soldier, (if the General will allow) ought to be stationed at the hospital, to take charge of the arms, &c. of the sick, whilst in the hospital, and to give them up on his death or dismission.

A Carpenter, ought to attend constantly, to make coffins, or perform other work, for which you will apply to the Quartermaster-General.

No blankets, or other effects of the Hospital, to be expended at the funeral of those soldiers, who die in the hospital.

I remain, Sir, your most humble servant,

JOHN MORGAN.

To JOHN WARREN, *Esquire,*
Surgeon in the General-Hospital.

The above is a true Copy, from the original.

J. WARREN.

WHEN General Green, as already related, removed from Long-Island, on account of the dangerous state

state of his health, General Sullivan was appointed to succeed him in the command; on which I thought it my duty to communicate to him, the plan observed in the government of the General Hospital, and for the regulation of the Regimental Surgeons, and to acquaint him with the above instructions to Dr. Warren, and the mode in which he managed his department; and wrote him a letter on the subject, that he might the better retain the principal heads of the proceedings, in his memory, should he have any occasion to refer to them, in issuing out orders, respecting the sick and wounded, as the enemy were already on Long-Island; and some important engagement with them, expected daily. To which I received the following answer:

New-York, August 21, 1776.

SIR,

I Received your favour of yesterday; am much pleased with your plan, respecting the Surgeons; shall take care that it is in every respect carried into execution; and am, with respect,
Your most obedient Servant,
JOHN SULLIVAN.

To Doctor MORGAN, *Director-General of the Hospitals,* &c.

And now, whilst I am on the subject of orders issued by me, to the different Gentlemen, for the better management of the General Hospital, on whose care I was to depend principally, for their being carried into execution, I must take the liberty to observe, that were I to transcribe all I have delivered to them in writing only, for that purpose, it would require a separate volume.

To Doctor Foster, as being the eldest Surgeon, I wrote much and often; and have now before me, copies of various orders to him, in a series of letters, &c. of which

which I will only mention dates, and occasions, without detaining the reader with particulars. The first (without date) was on his setting out from Cambridge, about the latter end of March, or beginning of April, 1776, to establish a General Hospital, at New-York. The next, likewise from Cambridge, April 22d: The next was at New-York, on my setting out from thence, for the management of the Hospital in my absence, whilst I proceeded to Philadelphia, to apply to Congress for further instructions, though I came away without obtaining them, but not without application, and as long time of attendance, as the General would allow me. The next, were dated at New-York, August 5th, the 19th, the 23d, and 27th; and September the 9th. The next, was also at New-York, September the 13th, for the intended removal of the sick and wounded, to Newark, respecting the manner of their removal, and the provision to be made for them, on that occasion, and for taking care of them, by the way. The next are dated September 24, October 18, and 20; November 3d, and 6th; whilst he had the care and superintendance of the sick at Newark; and of December the 10th and 31st; and January the 10th, at Bethlehem, for removal to the east side of Hudson's River.

Numerous and particular are the directions, which, in like manner, I have delivered in writing, on various occasions, as well as verbally, to Doctors Warren, Adams, M'Knight, Turner, and Eustis, Surgeons in the General Hospital; on their being detached to different places, for the establishment of Hospitals, for the conveniency of the sick, in parts distant from each other, in which my directions were drawn up with consideration, and not in a careless, negligent, or perfunctory manner; for that was neither the way, in which I chose to do business myself, or to require others to perform it, who were subject to my authority.

I shall now explain another difficulty, to which I was often subjected.

IT was no unusual thing for Officers and Regimental Surgeons, on detached posts, wherever they happened to be stationed, though ever so distant from the main body of the army, whether on a march, or a retreat, to expect a General Hospital to accompany, or follow them in the rear; as if it were possible, like the Polypus, though cut up into ever so many pieces, that each part should instantly repullulate, and become an entire Hospital, properly furnished with every necessary accommodation, attendants, and conveniences, although amidst Highlands, alps, or a forsaken and wasted country, without any help or assistance from those who had the command; or, as if it were possible to save, or remove the weighty and cumbersome apparatus, every where, with as much expedition as they could retreat, and without any regard to the unfitness of the place for a General Hospital.

I hope no intention of disrespect will be imputed to me, when I am sometimes necessarily obliged to make use of the names of Gentlemen of rank, for whom I have a personal and due respect, in the course of relating facts, which the vindication of my conduct requires I should discuss, with all becoming freedom, I think it proper to guard against such a wrong supposition, on the present occasion.

At a time when I had formed General Hospitals at Newark, Hackinsack, North-Castle, Stanford, and Norwalk, all crowded with sick, to the number of near 4000 men; and of course, the Hospital Surgeons who were not numerous, stationed at various distances, through a space of near an hundred miles, were differently employed, I received a letter from General Heath, at Peck's-Kill; one of the places I have seen spoken of as well that could be thought of for a General Hospital, as well for want of accommodations as of a poor country, to support it: It bore date, November —, on which he observed, that there was neither Hospital, nor any one General Hospital S——

Q

that poſt ; that he received daily complaints from the Colonels of the ſeveral regiments, of the ſufferings and diſtreſſes of the Regimental ſick ; and that " the neglect of them, was likely to prove very prejudicial to the inliſtment of a new army."

From the ſimilarity of language in this letter, the complaints of officers concerning the ſufferings of the ſick, and the evil conſequences that were predicted, of their proving prejudicial to the inliſtment of a new army, I was apprehenſive of the latent influence, and was determined, if I could any ways prevent it, they ſhould not have it in their power to lay the fault at my door. I might, indeed, have remonſtrated to the General that it was the duty of the Regimental Surgeons to ſend their ſick, whom they could not take care of, to the neareſt branch of the General Hoſpital, wherever I thought it moſt convenient for fixing it, and which I never did, without firſt adviſing with the officers who were in chief command, that they might be properly taken care of : But inſtead of that, the General Hoſpital was expected to attend every movement of theirs, not ſo much for ſending their ſick into it, as to claim ſupplies from it, or Hoſpital Surgeons to attend their regiments as was ſometimes required whilſt they were abſent, and ſcattered through the neighbouring States, in purſuing the uniform ſcheme they conſtantly kept in view, of eſtabliſhing Regimental Hoſpitals, for which they explored diſtant towns, and retired to them with part of their ſick : Theſe places became an aſylum for idleneſs, riot and diſſipation, for when once they got into ſuch places, they were in no haſte to return, and the numbers that reſorted to them, increaſed amazingly.

On receipt of General Heath's letter, I determined to ride from North-Caſtle to Peek's-Kill, to wait upon him, and concert the neceſſary ſteps to be taken, for accompliſhing his deſire, which I did ; but firſt I repreſented to him, how impracticable the deſign of
having

having a General Hospital there was, unless convenient quarters were first in readiness; that the providing quarters for the reception of the men being in the Quartermaster General's department, was under General Heath's command, and not in my power; but if he would undertake to give such orders, as would be executed, for the appropriating and fitting up rooms and births, for 300 sick, and would enforce obedience to the orders of Congress, October 9th, to allow no Regimental Hospitals in the neighbourhood of the General Hospital; and would call on the Regimental Surgeons, to remain with their respective corps, agreeable to General Washington's pleasure, of November 5; and to make such regular returns of the sick, that I could know the state of them; ordering some attendants on the Hospital, that would be much wanted, I would forthwith send a detachment of the General Hospital to attend his commands. I acquainted him, that it would answer no purpose, but to bring unmerited reproach on the hospital, if Gentlemen were sent up to take charge of it, and, when they came, no quarters could be had for their accommodation, or that of the sick*.

That the nature of the establishment and management of a Military Hospital might be the better understood, I drew up, November 20, an account of whatever was necessary, for providing quarters and accommodations, furnishing of supplies, and for the regular admission, care and attendants on the sick, with the necessary reports to be made, from time to time, to conduct matters with regularity, and to discover who do their duty, and who neglect it; so that if complaints are made of the sufferings of the sick, it may be known where the fault lies, and how to correct it. These I enclosed in my letter to him.

In return, the General " thanked me by letter, approved of my care and attention, and commended my
plans

* See my complaints on this head, page 45.

...ons and directions; and, as General Sullivan had ... before, promised to take care that they were, in ... respect carried into execution."

Doctor Adams, and Doctor M'Knight, successively waited upon General Heath, by my desire, to request that he would order such quarters, for the sick at Peek's kill, as were necessary for a General Hospital, which they were to direct; but never could be provided with any proper accommodations, when they were ... but were obliged to cross the Highlands, to Fish-kill, is twenty miles off, before they could meet with any suitable place, for the reception and accommodation of the sick.

Of the clamours of Regimental Surgeons, from want of Medicines.

OF all the complaints that have been made in respect to the sufferings of the sick, none have been so loud and clamorous as those proceeding from a want, or pretended want of medicines. I proceed, therefore, to examine into the nature and causes of those complaints, and I doubt not, to be able to convince the impartial world and Congress itself, that whether or not the Gentlemen, that compose that illustrious body, can justly exculpate themselves from the charge of neglect, in not providing the necessary supplies of medicines, for the Regimental Surgeons, and furnishing them therewith is left as to be of use to them. I am free from any merited blame on that account. And I wish the reader to remark that the complaints, on account of the sufferings of the sick, from want of medicines, were but mere whispers before the battle and retreat from Long-Island, compared to the clamours from that time forwards.

From the day of that retreat, August 28, 1776, a dreadful scene of confusion and disorder took place, which had a particular effect in disjointing all the measures of the Regimental Surgeons, and involving the

affairs

affairs of the General Hospital department, so far as it was complicated therewith, in the greatest difficulties, for the remainder of the year.

These misfortunes were increased by the obstinacy of the Regimental Surgeons in withstanding the orders of Congress; in which they were still supported by officers, who, to put the most favourable construction on their motives, were either not acquainted with the determinations of Congress respecting them, or not skilful in the duties of Regimental Surgeons, and the nature of Military Hospitals; or they were owing to the want of a proper arrangement in settling the duties of the Regimental Surgeons, and providing them with the proper means of discharging those duties. This may be imputed to the vast variety of business, that constantly occupied the Congress, which did not leave them sufficient leisure to attend to them, or their not sufficiently understanding the subject, from the defect of experience, on the first raising of an army; whereas they ought to have been early provided with medicines, instruments and bandages, by a Continental Druggist, or chosen Committee, before the campaign began: And the militia which came late to the field, should have been provided by the different States, before they joined the army: Some of them did not come till just before, and many not till after the retreat from Long-Island; and then came wholly unprovided with those articles, at a time when it was impossible, if there had been ever so great a plenty of medicines in the hospital or army subject, as both were, to continual movements, and when the officers of the hospital were divided, and as busily employed as men could be in taking care of the sick and wounded, to dispense them out to all applyers.

I early foresaw that this evil might happen, and as early pointed it out to the General, in the month of February, for the sake of applying a remedy, and of not being burdened with the charge of it, as may be seen in my letter to him, page 32. The contents of this letter, tee, I also communicated to Congress, the first opportunity I had for doing it, in person, which was in June following.

And after the retreat from Long-Island, I described my own situation to them, and that of the Regimental Surgeons, in the liveliest terms I could, praying for farther assistance, and pointing out the means of it, without success, as my letters to different members of the Medical Committee, will abundantly prove; but all my applications, on this subject, were in vain. I never received the least assistance from them.

In my narrative to General Washington, from page 7, to page 12, I have described what pains I had been at, to make provision of medicines, for the Regimental Surgeons, and to have the mode of furnishing the supplies clearly and properly established.

To what I then wrote, I have now to add some further observations, to free me from any misrepresentation, on this head.

When I made an offer of my best services to the Medical Committee of Congress, to supply the Regimental Surgeons at New-York, with regimental chests, though not in my line of duty to do so; it was not because I wished for the employ, being already burdened with much more business than belonged to my place, but because I did not find that Congress had taken any step for the purpose; and was apprehensive, lest when the evil arising from the neglect thereof, should be more sensibly felt and complained of, the ill consequences of that neglect would be charged upon me; and I expected thereby to get rid of a still greater evil, with which I heard I was threatened, as I told the Committee, that of being called on to furnish the hospitals and regiments, in the northern department, with instruments, medicines, &c. a thing impracticable in my situation, and in the exhausted state of America in respect to them. And I still expected, if Congress accepted of my proposal, they would have appointed an

apothecary

apothecary for the army, distinct from the hospital; or to have had the medicines put up at Philadelphia, in proper chests for regiments, to be sent to camp, duly prepared, of which I left with the Committee a proper list for the purpose. But what is surprizing, they never gave me any answer to these proposals, so that notwithstanding I engaged in the business, I never was properly authorized, or assisted for the discharge of that slavish employment; although, it seems, I was answerable for the consequences of my offer, as though I had been enabled, in every respect, to perform it.

Far be it from me, to charge the Committee with neglect in this business. All I mean is to defend myself against any imputation. What answer did they ever give me on that subject? None, except what is contained in a resolve of Congress, July 17th, of which I knew nothing, till that month was nearly expired; for when I was obliged by the General's order to return to camp, they had come to no determination. Nor, do those resolves enjoin it as a duty: They only forbid the Regimental Surgeons to draw any thing from the hospital, except instruments and medicines.

That it was not the intention, however, of Congress, to give them a right to demand these, except, as mentioned in the printed letter, page 72, (a copy of which I had laid before the Committee in June,) in small quantities, only to serve them till they could be supplied from any neighbouring place, is evident from the following consideration.

The Congress had committed their stock of medicines at Philadelphia, into the hands of Mr. William Smith, and by a vote of theirs appointed him Continental Druggist, or Commissary of Medicinal Stores, for which they allowed him pay, equal to 50 dollars per month. What was I to conclude from hence, but that the Congress had seen fit, and proper it was it should have done it long before to relieve me from a task foreign to my station, and to provide a person on purpose

purpose to supply the wants of the Regimental Surgeons: And that this was their idea, will appear farther probable, if it may be supposed the mind of Congress was known to one of their Members, who, some time after this, in a letter he wrote to me, expresses himself as follows: " With respect to supplying the Regimental Surgeons with medicines, I am fully of opinion that the Directors cannot well attend to it, but the application ought to be to them, in the first instance, and they to sign orders on the Continental Druggist for so many chests as they shall judge necessary, and have the medicines afforted, as they shall think proper."

IN REGARD TO INSTRUMENTS; anxious to have it in my power to furnish the hospitals more plentifully, as I had found it necessary to increase the number of Hospital Surgeons and Mates, and to recruit my stock of medicines, which was almost wholly exhausted of capital articles. I sent Doctor Binney to Philadelphia, a gentleman of the hospital, in whose zeal and activity I placed great reliance, to forward to camp, with all dispatch, what medicines I had there of my own, and as much as he could procure from Congress, for I could not be sufficiently supplied at New-York. I enjoined him to use the utmost diligence to purchase instruments, if to be had, ready made, or to engage a workman to make a great number of sets, on my account. He soon informed me, by letter, that there were no instruments to be purchased at any rate; and that the only workman in the city that could make surgeon's instruments was engaged by Mr. Marshall, for the Congress; and that he could not undertake any work for me, for a long time to come. Is not this an additional proof that Congress, in their resolves of July 17th, did not intend to make me answerable for the supplying of Regimental Surgeons, either with medicines or instruments; or, if it was their intention that I should furnish them; why did they not enable me to do it? Or why did they deprive me of the means?

By

By much assiduity, Doctor Binney, who was detained near a month in Philadelphia, at length sent forward such a supply of medicines as he could procure, which was very different, however, from the list I had sent for, which arrived at Newark but a short time before the retreat from Long-Island. It was then unsafe to attempt, if not impracticable to get them over to New-York; on which account, till the army abandoned the city, and the hospital stores were all removed to Newark, they remained there, where they had been left, except some articles which were wanted to supply the General Hospital, formed at this time near Kingsbridge, towards which place the army had retreated. I fixed Mr. Cutting, Assistant Apothecary, at Newark, which I considered as the most convenient and proper place at the time, for storing the medicines I had collected there, and referred such Regimental Surgeons, as applied to me for medicines, to him. This being my magazine of all that were most valuable, or most in demand, I felt the loss more sensibly, when they were taken out of my hands, in so irregular a manner, as I have already described in the first part of this work.

IN no part of the vast variety of duty and fatigue that I went through, have I been so sensible of ILL TREATMENT, as in what related to the supplies of medicines and hospital stores, except the more shameful and injurious manner in which I was deprived of them. It is next to impossible, to describe the toils that myself, and most of the Gentlemen of the hospital, have endured in that business; and the injurious reflexions that have been cast upon me, for conducting this affair, in a way the most meritorious, is truly matter of astonishment, and only to be equalled by the treatment I met with from Congress, in return for all those services.

To judge of this matter clearly, it is necessary to call to mind the difficulties under which I laboured for want of sufficient help, to consider the scarcity and value of medicines, and how troublesome or impracticable to procure them, in quantity, in America. I found no large stock on hand, when I first took charge of the hospital, to supply the vast demands of an army, in which generally more is wasted than used: The strictest œconomy was also enjoined me, in supplying the wants of the hospital, however much the plan of Congress is now changed. It is worth observing here, that the first piece of business the Congress employed me in, after my appointment to the Director-Generalship, was to look over a list of medicines made out by my predecessor, and not a large one, to supply the immediate wants of the hospital: A Committee of Congress put it into my hands, not so much, as I could understand, to add to it, if I thought necessary, as to curtail it: What was said on the occasion, at least, looked that way. With such views, such wants, and such œconomy, demands were made on me, from all quarters of the army, and out of the army, to distant parts of the country. All the assistance Congress allowed by their original establishment to procure, assort, prepare and dispense medicines, was one apothecary It being impossible to perform this service, without further help, a mate had been employed before my arrival, and an assistant with little more than soldiers pay, whom I also found here on my arrival, and continued him in his place, without being allowed any other help, till the year was almost over; when the Congress by their third resolve of October 9, 1776, at once, enjoined me to furnish such further quantities of medicines and bedding, as I might judge expedient, and impowered another, at the same time, to deprive me of what I had, with toil and fatigue immense, collected, and saved from destruction.

To be ordered by the General to collect medicinal stores, in the manner already mentioned, and to be abused and calumniated for performing that duty; and after supplying chests to five battalions at Boston, near

fifty

fifty at New-York, and sent twenty more to the northern department, and furnished the hospitals at Long-Island, New-York, Newark, Hackinsack, and Kingsbridge; and when I made demands on the Continental Druggist, for a small supply, to assort what remained on hand, not to be furnished with that necessary supply, was hard to be born: And yet to be baited like a bear at the stake, with incessant demands, and made responsible for the clamours of the Regimental Surgeons, for all the wants of new troops daily arriving, without supplies, and for the sufferings of the sick, arising from their opposition to General Orders; and so artfully excited that if I was at the General Hospital, crys were raised because I was not at camp, and if at camp, that they could not meet me at the General Hospital, was not less intolerable. The same noise pervaded from the remotest towns in the neighbouring States, to which the Regimental Surgeons had conveyed the sick, beyond the reach of relief, to terrify and alarm the country. Nor were these circumstances sufficient to fill up the measure of my distress. The most affecting representations were made to the General, from the distance of several hundred miles, ascribing the misfortunes of the army, ready to mutiny at the northward, to me, when I had early acquainted Congress with their situation, and prayed for relief for them in vain, although no part of my care. And notwithstanding I had sent them what I could spare from my own stock, and officers to assist them, at the earnest request of the director; I never met with the least acknowledgment for these services from the Congress, but, on the contrary, the strangest and most uncival returns from the Secretary, only for presuming to inquire of him, concerning the nature of the appointments Congress had made in some other departments, for the care of the sick, that I might the better understand, and understanding, better perform my own duty. Can there be a more striking instance of ingratitude than I have met in the whole of

my

my treatment, where the obligations to shew me a very different one, for my attention to, and for the manner ...ncharging my trust, were neither small nor few.

I shall here relate an instance of insolent and injurious treatment met with, for what I had not done, in place of thanks for what I had done to serve the northern department. It is contained in a letter from a certain Parson David Avery to Doctor Lind, and forwarded by him to the General in September last; in which, after giving a high wrought description of the sufferings of the sick at the lakes, for want of medicines, he introduces this virulent aspersion: "Men of chief consideration, (says he) are more than uneasy on this head, and do not hesitate to speak freely of first rate characters, as the authors of those calamities, some blaming the Congress and some the Surgeon-General, (meaning the Director-General) of the American Army and some the Director of the Northern Department. For my part, continues this reverend calumniator, I will not say which of them is the most guilty, but this I will affirm, that great guilt lies at some one's door." Strange that a preacher of the gospel which breathes charity to all, and especially to strangers, should carry the poison of asps under his tongue and spout forth his venom at this indiscriminate rate, against persons whom he knows little of, as is the case at least of one that had nothing to do in this matter, but as an act of extra-official benevolence, and who, though oppressed, as he was, with the greatness of his own burden, strove to mitigate and lighten that of others! And such are the grateful returns made to him for it.

BUT a circumstance that happened at that time, which I think of the most consequence to explain fully to the public is the REMOVAL of part of the HOSPITAL STORES from New-York to Stamford, previous to

the

the evacuation of Long-Island, and from thence to the interior parts of Connecticut; as this tranfaction was laid hold of as a handle of cenfure againſt me, and induced the General, by one of his aids, to write to, and acquaint me with the miferable fituation to which the fick were reduced, and the clamours excited, as it was alledged (but without reaſon) for want of medicines, as fet forth in my narrative, page 12, and 13. I ſhall now prove the truth of what I there alledged; that it was by his Excellency's own order, that I ſhipped the ſtores which were fent to Stamford; and the ſending them from thence farther inland, was by his commands, of which I had no knowledge at the time, whence the General himfelf, and every other reaſonable perſon, muſt be fo far from condemning, that they cannot, in juſtice, but approve my conduct. This account will likewife evince the impracticability of what he afterwards infifted upon I ſhould comply with immediately; but will ſhew, at the fame time, that it was undertaken with all diligence, and executed with all poſſible difpatch.

Sanguine as the generality of men unexperienced in military operations were, that the ſtrength of our works, and fo large an army as we had, were fufficient to defend New-York, againſt all the force that could be brought againſt it; others, of better underſtanding and cooler judgment, had great abatements in their belief of it. At any rate, they concluded it was very poſſible the town might be deſtroyed by the ſhipping, whether a landing was effected or not. Had a ſhell fallen amongſt the combuſtible articles of medicines, the whole might be deſtroyed, to the irreparable loſs of the army. I therefore aſked the General what he thought of removing thofe articles that could be beſt ſpared for the preſent, and mentioned Stamford, as a place to which they might be eafily tranfported by water, and from whence they might, at any proper time, when wanted, be brought back either by water or land. He not only approved of the proposition for their removal, but ordered it to be carried into execution, as expeditiously as I could. At this time, being the month of August, I had as I imagined, supplied almost every regiment in the army, with medicine chests: But fresh demands occurring every day, and the want of a transport v. ssel, impeded the performance of the General's commands, for some weeks.

I being in the most violent heat of summer, and so the less wanted, I ordered the greater part of the rugs and blankets, the newest and best bedding, of which I had collected a very large stock, and a thousand sheets of which I had lately got to the amount of near two thousand, many of them new, and a number of new shirts, at New-York, to be set apart for the purpose; and a large quantity of heavy hospital furniture, some of the largest bell metal and iron mortars, a number of crates of vials and gally pots, the largest bottles, with the most bulky articles, and those in the least demand, as some hogsheads and casks of cascarilla, and other such particulars as we could best spare, to accompany them. To these, I ordered a share of whatever we had in so great a plenty, as not to fear being soon destitute of them, to be added, with a small assortment of chosen medicines, to be made up and kept together in one or two suitable boxes, as a reserve, most likely to be wanted, and the most easily to be got at, on any pressing occasion. In the mean while, the British troops landed at Long-Island, and many officers and some Surgeons, perhaps the very men, who were afterwards foremost in the clamour, for want of medicines, came to the hospital, and expressing their apprehensions for the safety, took upon them to be very importunate for the removal of the hospital stores. I met the Adjutant-General, and told him in what state they were, and as reports of some frigates being shortly expected to appear in the sound prevailed, I proposed, once more, to know the General's mind, with regard to the removal of the

stores:

stores: He told me he had heard the General express himself on the subject very lately, with wishes of their being gone; whereupon he, believing it to be so, informed him of such his assurance, that they were already sent away; and urged me to lose no time to have it done. A small transport being forthwith engaged, the abovementioned stores, amounting to eighteen tons, were immediately put on board, and sent off, under the care of Doctor Ledyard, of the hospital; they were safely landed at Stamford, and committed to the care of John Lloyd, Esq; of that place, who stored them in his own house.

An apprehension and alarm prevailing soon after, that the enemy were about to make a sudden descent upon that place, and might destroy the stores if not removed farther from the sound; Mr. Lloyd wrote to the General on the subject, and received his commands in return; in pursuance of which the Committee had them removed further into the interior country, and particularly the most valuable were conveyed to no less a distance than fifty miles, for safety; of which I had no notice at the time, but have since obtained a copy of the General's order for their removal, and a certificate from the Committee at Stamford, of their removal, in virtue of the General's said order, contained in the following letter.

To JOHN LLOYD, *Esquire, at Stamford.*

SIR, *New-York, August* 31, 1776.

I HAVE it in command from his Excellency General Washington, to acknowledge your favour of this date, and to request, in his name, that you will apply to the Committee of Stamford for assistance, to remove the stores in your possession, to such place or places as you and they may judge necessary for their security. Whatever expences shall attend their removal, will be punctually paid, as soon as the bill thereof is rendered. As these stores are of great use, and may

be

be of the utmost consequence, and things are so circumstanced here, that persons and carriages, proper to convey them, cannot be sent; his Excellency is hopeful you will excuse this trouble, and that yours and the Committee's kind exertions, will most readily be employed upon this occasion.

I am, Sir, your most obedient Servant,

ROB. H. HARRISON, Secretary.

A true Copy, JOHN LLOYD.

Long-Island was abandoned to the British troops, 3 days before the date of the above letter; and in less than 3 weeks more, New-York also fell into their hands. With difficulty could the remaining hospital stores be saved, by transporting them, over the North River to the Jerseys, and thence to Newark. And yet it was within ten days, from that time, and whilst I was taking measures to overlook and put in order the medicines, and to get a fresh list of capital articles, wanted to assort them, that, owing to the clamours beforementioned, I received that severe and unmerited reprehension, quoted in my narrative, page 13.

I wrote to Philadelphia for medicines, but could get none, or next to none. The Gentlemen, to whom I wrote, acquainted me their shops were exhausted. From the Continental Druggist I obtained a very small supply indeed, with a proper apology for it.

Under all these difficulties, I did not slacken my endeavours to obtain a supply. I sent through the different States of New-England, and applied, in person, to the State of New-York, at Fish-Kills, and, not long after, had hospitals established at Stamford and Norwalk, well supplied with medicines and other stores, the former of which, received into it above 12,00 patients, who were comfortably provided for, under the care of Doctor Philip Turner, most of whom recovered; and the latter above 700, under the care of Doctor Eustis:

Eustis; both of whom furnished, from the hospital, all Regimental Surgeons who applied, with whatever medicines they called for, to the full of their demands. By the exactest accounts and returns of the patients received into the hospital at Stamford, from November 5th, to the time of my dismission being known there, in February following, the amount was near thirteen hundred, of whom the number, remaining in the hospital, was then reduced to twenty-five, in all. Doctor Eustis informed me, that upwards of seven hundred sick and wounded were well provided for, by means with which I had sufficiently furnished him, whom he was enabled to attend, much to their satisfaction; and that when he left Norwalk, in March, the number remaining was reduced to eight or ten.

The GOVERNOR of CONNECTICUT has also favoured me with the following testimonial of my application to him for assistance, and of the good effect of it.

BE IT KNOWN,

That in the beginning of October, 1776, Doctor John Morgan, then Director-General of the Hospitals, of the American Army, made application to me, by letter, for my assistance, in supplying the troops of the State of Connecticut, with medicines and other necessaries for their sick; mentioning the general want thereof, and his inability (without some aid of this kind) to answer the numerous demands daily made on him, and the consequent distress of the sick and wounded of the army. In compliance with which request, I immediately sent Doctor Philip Turner, with a quantity of necessary articles to his assistance, and by this means the complaints of the soldiery were greatly lessened.

JONATHAN TRUMBULL, Governor of the State of Connecticut.

Lebanon, April 7, 1777.

WERE it neceffary to produce other evidences of the pains I took to acquaint Congrefs of the fuffering condition of the fick, I could refer to a number of letters I have written to feveral of the members, containing a particular hiftory of the movements of the hofpitals and fick, during the whole campaign, particularly to Mr. Gerry, Member for Maffachufetts-Bay, and Doctor Rufh, of Philadelphia, and efpecially in a letter I wrote to the former, October 6th.

In that letter I informed him " of the great clamours that prevailed, at the time, amongft the Regimental Surgeons, becaufe they could not be fupplied with every thing they wanted, from the General Hofpital, of which I gave him a full and juft reprefentation. It contained, likewife, a long and particular relation of all my proceedings in the care of my department, from the time I entered into the fervice, to that period, conformable to what I have delivered in my narrative to General Wafhington. I pointed out to him the ftate of the Regimental Surgeons, ever fince I entered into the fervice, and the deftitute condition they were in, at my firft arrival in the army, in refpect to all forts of ftores, inftruments and medicines. I acquainted him with the pains I had been at, to furnifh them with neceffaries, and the extent to which I had done it, with my applications to the General and Congrefs to fettle the channels of fupply, and with the applications to me from Canada, for that purpofe. I let him know, that I had fent off to the amount of twenty regimental chefts, for the troops at Lake George and Albany, befides what I had fent to General Gates at Ticonderoga, (exclufive of betwixt forty and fifty regimental medicine chefts, fupplied to the forces under the immediate command of General Wafhington,) and acquainted him with what had been fent by the General's order to Stamford."

" I further gave him as exact a defcription, as it was in my power, of the ftate of the fick and wounded, and of the unufual complaints amongft the militia ; of
the

the continual vicissitude in the state of the sick, from the various movements of the army, and consequent shiftings of the hospital; and of the difficulties to which this reduced the officers employed in attending it; of the necessity we were under to remove the stores and sick to Newark; and the obstacles we had to overcome, under many inconveniences, to convey them to a place of safety, and to provide them with quarters; and withall, I told him of the unruly behaviour of the surgeons of the militia regiments, and their tumultuous applications for medicines; and informed him how widely they were scattered through the country; of the desertion of some of the Regimental Surgeons, and the calls on the Mates of the Hospital to supply their places."

"I concluded my letter to him with the following observations: "Upon the whole matter, it appeared to me, that a general mistake prevailed concerning the duty of the Regimental Surgeons, and the manner in which they ought to be furnished with instruments, medicines and necessary stores. I gave it as my opinion, in the most express terms, that they ought not to depend on the General Hospital for them, because, in its present exhausted condition, and the loose state in which every thing was, from the scattered condition of the sick, and the vast variety of duty, and infinite fatigue of the department, it was impossible for me to furnish the Regimental Surgeons, and not essentially injure, or totally overthrow the General Hospital. And observed to him, that whilst there was such a limitation in the number of surgeons and other officers in the hospital, and the Regimental Surgeons could claim any right to depend upon it for supply of what they required, it must soon be entirely exhausted of the means of answering its design, and be rendered wholly useless. I therefore recommended to Congress, the appointment of proper persons, to look out, and purchase medicines sufficient for a store to be formed at Philadelphia, from whence what might be wanting for regimental

mental use, could be sent up in proper chests to every Regimental Surgeon, as his occasions required."

"Thus, I observed, being somewhat more disengaged from the present innumerable calls on me, that were foreign to my duty, I should enjoy more leisure for what were proper to my station, and then would sketch out some further plan for the better government of the General Hospital and Regimental Surgeons, and the best means of furnishing the needful supplies." And, soon after, I sent such a list of medicinal stores and surgeons instruments, &c. as I concluded would be necessary for an army of 20,000 men, for a twelvemonth, including both hospitals and regiments.

I accordingly drew up the above mentioned plan in a few days after, by the General's Orders; which being first submitted to his remarks, and those of Lord Sterling, and of General M Dougall, as it was agreed upon, was then forwarded shortly after, by General M'Dougall, to General Green, that his remarks being added, it might be returned to me, with all dispatch, to compare the whole, and revise it for laying before the Congress.

As General Green had shewn so much zeal in the affair, and had made such warm representations, successively, to General Washington, and to the President of the Congress, on the subject, setting forth, that if the present evil was not quickly remedied, it would fatally injure the service: I did not doubt, that he would give it all possible dispatch, and send it to me, so soon as he could examine it. But although I wrote, and sent message after message, I could never get it again, till a few days before Christmas, when I called on him for it, in person, and received it, without the benefit of a single observation of his, to accompany its return. However, I sat down, so soon after as I could, and reduced the whole into eight articles, which I enclosed to Mr. Samuel Adams, to lay before Congress, with two sheets of paper, containing remarks, and reasons in support

port of them. Of these, together with what I had communicated to the Committee, at my conference with them in June, and to several of the Members, in my letters to the President and others, I find they have not disdained to make great use, in the arrangements which have since taken place, on a very large scale, and especially in what related to the arrangement of the superior officers, and the subordination they have traced out in the department.

I have not mentioned Gen. Green's omission to perform what he undertook, from believing it to be voluntary; but as some persons, who having no better reason at hand to assign for my removal, have, it seems, charged me, with having promised to lay some plan before Congress, for better regulating the department, and having then neglected it for near three months, during which time, many of the evils complained of, continued without redress, I thought it became me to give a true relation of the cause of that delay, so far as it respected myself. I doubt not General Green's being able to give such substantial reasons for his delaying to perform his promise, as will be fully satisfactory: But as that regards him more than myself, I leave it to him to state this matter as he pleases, if he should chance to think the taking notice of it at all, to be worthy of his attention.

BESIDES the afore-described letter to Mr. G— written with a view to give Congress all necessary information of the state of my department, and every thing that had a relation to it, to awaken their attention to the state of the sick and Regimental Surgeons, as well as the hospital department, to make what reformations and amendments in it they thought proper, I wrote a letter to Dr. Rush, a Member of the Medical Committee; and from the same motive, my anxiety on account of the sufferings of the sick, to rouse the attention of Congress to make this matter a

serious

ferious fubject, before they should be compelled to do it, from being overtaken with those calamities which too soon after came on, and, with the rapidity of a torrent, swept away many hundreds, if not thousands, into the ocean of eternity.

Although it is a long letter, and contains repetitions of matters, some of which I have already mentioned, more than once; yet on that very account, of their being repetitions, they have their use; and the length of my letter, at a time when I had so much to claim my attention, is a proof that my mind was deeply engaged in the subject: They carry with them the most convincing evidence, that if the sick suffered, as they indisputably did, more than might be expected, had the Congress done their part, either in making the necessary provision, before the campaign began, or understood how to regulate matters rightly at first; or had been as attentive, in applying seasonable remedies, as I was, to point out the disorders and means of redress, it was not owing to any neglect of mine, or any fault that I have yet been reproached with, from want of experience or abilities for the task, or of zeal and activity in discharging my duty: But of this, let the impartial judge. The letter is as follows:

To Doctor BENJAMIN RUSH.
Member of the Medical Committee of CONGRESS.

SIR, *Hackinsack, Oct.* 20, 1776.

BY command of General Washington, all the sick and wounded, both in the General Hospital, and those remaining under the care of Regimental Surgeons, are removed within these two days, to this side the river, and chiefly in this neighbourhood: They amount to several hundreds, in addition to about 300 who were before removed to Newark, and 4 or 500 in Orange County. I have neither Commissary near at hand, nor Quartermaster, and brought with me only

three

three Mates: One Surgeon who was to follow, is hourly expected. The General's commands were to leave a respectable body of Surgeons and Mates above Kingsbridge, a general action being daily expected, as the whole force of the enemy is drawn to that quarter. So soon as I get this part of the General Hospital into order and regularity, I am to return, and provide accommodations at the White Plains, for which indeed I gave the necessary orders before I came over, that in case the communication by the North-River should be cut off, for a while, which no doubt the enemy mean to attempt, suitable provision may be made for the wounded, should there be a general action, which is daily expected. I wrote to Mr. Gerry, giving an account of the state of the hospital, since the affair of Long-Island which I wish you to see. My anxiety to preserve hospital stores occasioned my removal of the heavy articles to Stamford, which I effected, just in time to prevent their falling into the enemy's hands. Great part of what remained at New-York, were again divided, part to be removed to Kingsbridge, with the Hospital Surgeons and Mates, who remained with the army; the rest to be sent with the sick to Newark. In packing and unpacking medicines, and dealing them out, with other hospital stores, to Regimental Surgeons and Mates, near one half of our mates of the hospital have been employed the whole summer and autumn, to this time, to the mere subversion, and almost total destruction, of the General Hospital. We are now scarcely any thing more than collectors and retailers to Regimental Surgeons and Mates; and the stores are so divided, wasted, and dissipated, that without a new arrangement, and abundant more assistance than we have, or can have, or the hospital continuing fixed in one place, we shall shortly be incapable of yielding any assistance at all. The greatest difficulty is the supplying medicines to the whole army. Think how I came to have that charge, in addition to my duty as Director-General, &c. and that it was only

designed

designed as a temporary expedient; and consider the difficulties and inconveniences of continuing to execute it, and you must soon be convinced how impracticable it is for me to answer the intention. When I first arrived in the army, I found the Regimental Surgeons destitute of medicines, instruments, and bandages; therefore a useless set, in case of action. I represented this to General Washington, and pointed out to him the necessity of every regiment being supplied, the ensuing campaign, with a medicine chest for the whole year: But where to get the medicines was the question, or who was to fit out the Surgeons. I recommended an application to Congress, to employ some one in Philadelphia, to provide chests for each regiment. Whilst matters were under consideration, Boston was evacuated by the British troops: By dint of unwearied assiduity, I collected a great number of blankets, beds and rugs, which had been left, by the British army, in hospitals, barracks, and in the river: I had them washed, and made fit for use. By the General's Orders I took possession of a large Druggist's shop, and a small one of a private practitioner, after they were gleaned of capital articles, as camphor, rhubarb, bark, opium, &c. The General concluding it would be a means of supplying the regiments, as well as General Hospital, ordered me to purchase such articles as were wanted, and as I could get, and make out chests for every regiment, in the army which he commanded: This made it late before I could get to New-York, and above half the mates were employed, in packing and accompanying the medicines to New-York. Hearing, on my arrival, that the Congress had a large assortment of medicines at Philadelphia, and being called upon by the surgeons, in the northern department, to supply them, I hastened to Philadelphia to confer with a Committee of Congress, and have my duty better ascertained: I found that of a valuable assortment of capital articles, which the Congress had purchased, there had been considerable deductions

for

for the use of the southern army, and part sold, as if the quantity was greater than was required for public use: On which I represented to the Committee the necessity of husbanding the stock well. I begged that a share might be appropriated for the use of the army under General Washington, and undertook to furnish for the present campaign, the regiments of that army, with chests for the campaign, not imagining they would exceed the number of 40 regiments, especially as the Flying Camp was to form a separate department; and was fearful left, if regiments were unequally served, great part of the Surgeons would be destitute and useless. To make out the better, I bought up all the valuable articles I could meet with at New-York, and elsewhere: Besides 5 regiments which I supplyed with chests at Boston, and 20 to the northward, I supplyed, from the beginning of July to the middle of August, above 40 chests. Then fresh demands came from hosts of militia, the numbers countless, who joined the army, destitute of every thing necessary for sick and wounded, as instruments, bandages, or medicines: They demanded even their provisions, as well as medicines, from me, and our whole force of Surgeons and Mates were chiefly employed to furnish the Regimental Surgeons: The labour was too great, the task beyond our abilities, for medicines became more scarce every day, and our stores dissipated. The making provision, to save part of our stores, before the affair of Long-Island, and the confusion in which we have been ever since, moving about by detachment; the sick scattered, under the care of Regimental Surgeons, for a tract of 30 miles and upwards; only one apothecary being allowed; no leisure for either him or me to leave the army, and look out for supplies; and none to be got for writing, or next to none; the wounded requiring our care; destitute of help from Quartermasters and Commissaries, when removed to a distance; All concur to shew that the resolve of Congress, that the Directors shall supply medicines to the Regimental Surgeons,

Surgeons, is a thing impossible, at least in my department, for any length of time, unless I am allowed to leave the camp, and range through the different States, or rather to employ a variety of persons for that purpose. I have represented the matter to the General, and now hope the Congress will take it into consideration. I have been reduced to the necessity of sending a surgeon to proceed through New-England, to collect medicines, as Doctor Stringer is gone in person, for his department. I have wrote to Governor Trumbull and the Assembly of Connecticut, for their assistance ; to the State of New-York for help ; sent for and issued out all my own stock of medicines ; purchased from public bodies, and private practitioners ; wrote to Mr. Bass, Mr. Smith and others : All is insufficient. I shall make out another list, and send to Mr. Smith ; but I fear much that I shall not get what I want, in Philadelphia : It is distressing to the last degree, to be harrassed with such unceasing clamorous demands, for what I neither have, nor can get ; and if I had them, I have not help sufficient to issue them out, it being as much as two or three persons can do to prepare, and issue out medicines for the sick in the General Hospital, diffused as ours is, and necessarily so.

General Washington has ordered me to draw up a plan for the government of the General Hospital, and of the Regimental Surgeons, such as I think practicable in the execution, and best calculated to answer the design of both : I presented him with a rough sketch, which he has examined, and made his remarks : Lord Sterling has done the same ; and it is now in the hands of General M'Dougall ; and it is to pass through General Green's, then to undergo corrections and amendments, to lay before the Congress, for which this may prepare you.

This minute I learn, that the British troops have withdrawn from Frog's-Point ; are landed at New Rochell ;

a general action is hourly expected; an important event, on which much depends.

The design of this letter is, principally, to prepare the attention of Congress to the affairs of my department. We want rags, old linnen, bandages, lint, tow, thread, needles and pins, &c. They are not to be got here. Would it not be worth the attention of a Committee of Congress, or some active Members, to set some inhabitants of the city to collect these, and other necessary articles, and send off with dispatch. They cannot come too soon, or in larger quantity than sufficient. The hospital has been drained by supplying Regimental Surgeons. We must depend on the public to furnish fresh supplies: They are not to be got here: I am overwhelmed with business; I cannot leave the hospital to go in search of them. *I now give notice of my difficulties, while I can, in time, that in case of falling short of the quantity of those necessaries, I may not be blamed for the impossibility of collecting them.*

I shall inclose you a list of medicines wanted for such an army as General Washington's, which I conceive to be rather moderate than extravagant. Without so capital a stock is provided in time, we shall be unfurnished for another campaign: Nor do I think it sufficient for more than six such months as the last. Judge then whether it will not be necessary to employ Commissaries to purchase medicines; to prepare them before they come to the army; to provide a place of safety, at a proper distance from danger, and not subject to continual movements; to have an Apothecary for the army or regiments, distinct from the Hospital Apothecary, and mates and labourers to assist in issuing them out, when wanted, to the respective Surgeons. I remain,

Sir, your most humble Servant,
JOHN MORGAN.

The Public may desire to know what was the effect of the above representation and earnest application for
some

(148)

some relief. There are few, perhaps, but readily conclude, that this notice of my difficulties produced immediate and powerful assistance; or, that the Congress did me ample justice, in exculpating me from all censure and blame for want of ▆▆. Quite the contrary of all this is the fact. No m▆▆e notice was taken of this information, that ever came to my knowledge, than if it were a tale of what happened in ages past, that did no ways concern ourselves.

When the remnant of the army that retreated from Brunswick had crossed the Delaware, I proceeded to Philadelphia, to wait on Congress, and to lay matters before them in person, for such regulations for the better care of the sick and wounded, as were suitable to the occasion, and to obtain an explanation and amendment of the resolves of Congress, October 9th. I met Doctor Rush in the street, and attempted, for a moment, to detain him, till I could acquaint him with the present circumstances, and situation of affairs: He gave me no time: All he said was, that "he was glad I was come; it would take a great burden from his shoulders," and passed on. When I afterwards called upon him, at his house, to represent matters to him there, as a Member of the Medical Committee, for relief; the sum of his answer was, that "he would not, for ten times the consideration, go through the amazing toils and difficulties of my station." But instead of relief from the difficulties and hardship of my situation, all the returns I received from Congress, are complaints disregarded, grievances unredressed, and, without an hearing, and without assigning a reason, a dismission from my station, as if Congress intended to fix a stigma on my character. But however hidden the motives for such conduct are, a day may come, when these will be fully understood.

The same Gentleman who then felt, or seemed to feel for my situation, having since accepted a place, near of kin to that which he then so earnestly deprecated, may perhaps remember it. I can truly say, should he aspire

to,

to, or hereafter enjoy, that very place, I do not wish him the ill-treatment and ingratitude for his services in it, which I have experienced.

TO SHEW how difficult it was for me to receive any exact information from Congress, on such particulars as I conceived it necessary to know, I need only acquaint the reader with the following particulars.

Being applyed to by Doctor Potts, who acted in the character of Director in a separate branch of the northern department, to send him proper persons, to assist him, otherwise it would not be in his power to discharge the trust reposed in him, I nominated two gentlemen for that purpose, in the quality of a Surgeon, and Apothecary to that part of the hospital.

As other demands of that sort might be made upon me, I wrote to Mr. Charles Thomson, Secretary, requesting him to acquaint me, from the Journals of the Congress, whether the nomination of Surgeons to fill up vacancies, in any part of the General Hospital of the northern department, rested with me, as Director-General and Physician in Chief of the American Hospital. It appeared, that Doctor Stringer had been impowered to take charge of the northern department, the nature of which I did not fully understand: But I thought the resolves of July 17, last, warranted me to call upon him, as one of the Directors, for returns of surgeons, mates, and other officers, &c. but then he had wrote word to me, that he conceived himself to be a senior officer, and upon a supposition of our ever coming together, expected precedence, from that priority, or to take rank of me; and had given me to understand in express terms, that he never would be accountable to me, or to any person, but the Commander of the particular department where he was, or to the Commander in Chief: And referred me to the votes of Congress, September 14, for the particulars of his appointment.

Having

Having no access to those votes otherwise, I informed the Secretary, in the letter which I wrote him, of my desire to avoid interfering with Doctor Stringer, in his department, from any misconception of the intentions of Congress; and asked as a favour, that he would be pleased to let me have a copy of the votes, relative to Doctor Stringer's appointment and instructions, and to Doctor Shippen's appointment and instructions, that I might know whether it was the duty of those Gentlemen to make me the specified returns of July 17th, or not.

Did he comply with my request? Or what answer did this *polite, obliging* Secretary, return me, and two other Gentlemen, Members of Congress, to whom I also wrote to request they would second my application to him for copies of the votes and instructions, &c.? He sent them not, but in place thereof, in a positive magisterial way, gave me to understand, (in which however, he was greatly mistaken) that "*undoubtedly* at the appointment of those Gentlemen, they had the same powers given to them, *in all respects*, of nominating their own surgeons, nurses, &c. in their department I had myself in mine; and as to rank and precedence, and all that nonsense (as he called it) was nothing in the Journals to establish it."

By this time, I had obtained from Doct. himself a copy of his appointment, and of the power vested in him by Congress, Sept. 14, 1775 (p. 27) which enabled me to point out his mistake, shewing him that Doctor Stringer had no power given him, by those resolves, of nominating the Surgeons, or any officers whatever, except his mates, not to exceed four; a power not derogatory in any way of the Surgeons, appointed by me; and I assumed a power of nominating five mates; and I also took the liberty to tell this GREAT MAN that as it concerned me to be well acquainted with, for the direction of my conduct, I preferred a state of facts to gloffes, on which I could form a judgment of my own on the evidence they afforded; and that had he been

pleased

pleased to have examined these resolves of Congress, his disobliging observations on rank and precedence, might have been spared; I further told him, that men bred up in the army, had different notions from what he seemed to entertain, and that supposing their rank and their pay were to come into competition with each other, every officer of spirit and honour, would rather sacrifice his pay, as of less consequence, than his rank; and then asked him, if it was a matter of no importance, how it came to pass that the Congress, in their late resolves, had determined that the surgeons and mates of the hospital should take rank of regimental surgeons and mates.

His letter, in reply to this, contained in it several expressions so rude, and impertinent to the matter in hand, that I chuse to omit them; but he very cynically observed, that "having never been conversant in courts or camps, he doubted not that his way of thinking, (as if that were to be the standard, and supercede the votes of Congress, of which he ought to have considered himself the servant, and not the master) might appear as old fashioned to them, as their proceedings, at times, appear ridiculous to him, where rank stands for merit, and that fantastical thing ca'led honour, (with which, by his invectives on it, he gives room enough to suppose he is little acquainted) supplys the place of virtue;" and concluded with a rhapsody on Commonwealths, that I conceived to be very foreign to the subject, as I never asked for a display of his principles, having barely requested such information of the resolves of Congress as might enable me to know, and to discharge my duty, the better. I only wished to guard against breaking down those barriers, which were most likely to secure my rank and authority from innovations upon them; and which, perhaps, this very Gentleman might be instrumental in introducing, afterwards, into the votes of October 9th, which I conceived I had so much reason to complain of, as the first approach that was made to undermine my
commission.

commission, which however could not be thoroughly effected, without attempting likewise to blow up my reputation, though unsuccessfully.

THAT I may at length bring this detail and examination of facts to a conclusion, I shall make some abstracts from several certificates and testimonials, presented to me by the Gentlemen of the General Hospital who have accidentally fallen in my way, since the affair of my dismission happened, which has enabled me to obtain their sentiments on the subject.

These abstracts set forth, that on being called upon for the purpose, and considering themselves in honour obliged to certify facts of which they are acquainted, respecting the conduct and management of JOHN MORGAN, Esq; late Director-General of the American Hospital, and Physician in Chief, from being officers in said hospital, and therefore falling under their cognizance.

To ALL WHOM IT MAY CONCERN

They testify,——That the said JOHN MORGAN, gave orders to the different Surgeons of the General Hospital, to receive under their care all patients belonging to the army, whether sick or wounded, that were duly reported and found to be proper objects, without distinction, with full power to draw on the said department for whatever medicinal and other stores could be procured—That the said Director-General was ever attentive to any calls which they made upon him, for the supply of the hospital, and for procuring comfortable accommodation, provision, necessaries and refreshments for the sick—That in particular instances, on the breaking up of Regimental Hospitals, and routing of the sick, by the approach of the enemy, the sick being poured upon his care in vast numbers, without either Surgeon, Mate, Quartermaster, or any one officer to accompany: Doctor MORGAN having but little

assistance

affiſtance for ſuch amazing and ſudden increaſe of numbers, went from houſe to houſe, to procure quarters for the ſick, and proviſion for their ſupport; inſtructing the Country People in what manner to take charge of them, even to ſeeing them provide their meals for preſent refreſhment, and take care for their future ſuſtenance—That he viſited the hoſpitals, going through each ward in perſon, to ſee that the ſick were duly attended, and provided for—That he conſulted very readily with the Surgeons, and gave his aſſiſtance whenever there was occaſion, and ſhewed a readineſs to remove any difficulty that offered to the utmoſt of his power—That he performed capital operations himſelf, when preſent, or aſſiſted the Surgeons of the hoſpital therein, and hath ſtooped to do the duties of a mere mate, in dreſſing the moſt ſimple, as well as the moſt dangerous wounds of the ſoldiers in the General Hoſpital, as an example and encouragement to the officers under him, to attend carefully to that duty—That if the ſick have at any time ſuffered more than uſual, it has been from unavoidable accidents, not in his power to remedy—That there were no complaints of the ſick ſuffering in the General Hoſpital under their care; but that the uneaſineſs which aroſe was, concerning the care and proviſion of thoſe who were retained in their regiments, and not reported to the General Hoſpital—That they have been witneſſes to his conſtant application and attention to the duties of his ſtation, in which his diligence, aſſiduity, care of, and humanity towards the ſick and wounded, were abundantly evident—That the principal cauſes of the ſufferings of the ſick, the laſt campaign, proceeded from the regimental ſick not being properly reported to the General Hoſpital, and, in ſome inſtances, to the unavoidable ſcarcity of particular medicines and other ſtores, which could not be procured, at all times, in ſufficient quantities, and not, ſo far as ever came under their notice, to any want of care and attention in the Director-General; but principalpally from the repeated movements of the army, which exposed the sick and wounded to sufferings that could in no ways be remedied, under those circumstances—And are firmly of opinion, that no person whatever, acting in the station of Director-General, under the same circumstances, could possibly have given universal satisfaction."

THE above abstracts are taken from certificates signed by John Warren, Philip Turner, and William Eustis. Esquires, Surgeons of the General Hospital, and Isaac Ledyard, Esq; Apothecary to the General Hospital, in the Eastern Department. Doctor Foster was generally detached, and at a distance. I have never seen Doctors Adams, M'Knight, or Burnet, since my dismission, to converse with them on the subject; but have no doubt of meeting with equal readiness in them, to testify to the same faithful discharge of my duty, with the other Gentlemen, whenever they are called upon for that purpose. But what occasion is there for further evidence. To accumulate it, would, in my opinion, be as unnecessary as to hold up torches to the sun.

" *When Phœbus does his beams display,*
" *To tell me gravely, that 'tis day,*
" *Is to suppose them blind.*"

It may not be improper to say a few words, respecting the Gentlemen who have acted immediately under me; one of whom is raised to the rank of Deputy Director General; None of them, that I know of, have done discredit to their places.

However Congress may reconcile it to themselves, and to the justice that is supposed to be due to Gentlemen of unexceptionable characters, that have served them faithfully, and with approved ability, from the beginning of the war; and have deserved well at their hands, for what they have done and suffered, from being constantly engaged as Surgeons in the General Hospital, since its first establishment; to pass them by, and to place over their heads some who were never before in the service, and others who were their juniors; they have, however unintentionally, done great honour to my appointments. Of three Gentlemen whom I nominated, and who have served under me, as Surgeons, who are all I ever appointed, and were the youngest in the hospitals of my department, two of them are promoted, by Congress, to the stations of Physician General, and Surgeon General, in the Army. Can a stronger proof be given of the care and fidelity with which I exercised that trust, than in employing, as officers under me, Gentlemen whom the Congress itself has seen fit, since, to distinguish in so extraordinary a manner? And when one of the beforementioned Gentlemen, who had just reason to expect to be noticed amongst the first appointments in the department, was for some time, at least, wholly overlooked, by them, as he was to my knowledge, probably, because he could not consent to be troubling Congress, either by himself or friends, with solicitations in his behalf, though they were not ignorant of his services; and though brother to HIM, who laid down his life in their CAUSE, and whose memory is held sacred by them; but who, without deriving merit from any extrinsic or adventitious circumstances, has conducted himself in a manner that reflects honour upon his talents and humanity!

If Congress could be capable then, of so long neglecting the known, but modest worth of Doctor JOHN WARREN, the world may less wonder they should so easily get over the obligations they owed to myself, and to their own reputation.

As to the Mates, many of them are raised to the rank of Surgeons of Regiments, and I doubt not, that by their superior knowledge in the duties of their station, above what many of their predecessors enjoyed, they will reflect credit on the General Hospital, under my direction, as a School to qualify them for superior services.

As to myself, and the unworthy treatment I have met with; I call it unworthy; for so it is, in respect to me, however worthy it may be of the authors of it, whatever credit and growing fame some may imagine they have acquired by it, I consider it not as any dishonour to me, but to those only who have procured it. Time, the great revealer of Mens motives as well as actions, will perhaps, one day, unmask the private and disguised designs of men, who cover them at present, with a pretext of public good, but which are visible by their actions to the quicker sight of discerning men, who judge of a tree, not by its appearances, but its fruits. I do not envy them, but rather wonder, and wish them to enjoy the just reward of their devices.

"*Nec Drances potius, sive hæc est ira deorum,*
"*Mo te luat, sive est virtus aut gloria, tollat.*"

I doubt not, but they will fail, however, in one part of their design, and by endeavouring to throw an odium on my character, fix an indeliable mark on their own; and, perhaps, find that injustice so sweet to their taste, may, before it is digested, bring forth gaul and bitterness, and what they have sowed in deceit and folly, they may reap in remorse and disappointment.

Leaving them, therefore, to the opinion which the juster and wiser part of mankind may have of them in this proceeding, and to the operation of that inward monitor in their own breasts, I am satisfied in having hung out lights to those embarked in the same bottom with designing men, who steering amidst rocks and quick-sands, "hold themselves in readiness to plunder the vessel they mean to wreck."

I have endeavoured to discharge my duty in what I undertook from principle, according to my degree of knowledge and capacity, with faithfulness and diligence; and what I value more than knowledge or capacity alone, with humanity; from whence results the approbation of a good conscience, which as my enemies, with

all

all their power, cannot give, so neither can they take away. Why then should I repine at the portion of difficulties, that, in times like these, have fallen to my lot, and which I have neither coveted, nor been able to shun? Having been born in freedom, I claim it, in common with every other freeman, as an indisputable, unalienable right, which I have never surrendered to any one, to defend my good name from the attacks of insidious men, of whatever class or denomination. Be it ever, therefore, my part to declare, without fear and without reserve, that true Freedom is my "unconquerable delight," and that I am equally a foe to false pretences of Liberty, and "to every species of bondage," but most to "that of the mind."

As to those who have made themselves busy to reflect on my character, I consider their envy to be rather a proof of merit, than dread the power of their malice to affect me, since, in every age,

"*Envy does merit, as its shade, pursue,*
"*And by the shadow, proves the substance true.*"

But neither pretending, nor wishing, to derive any merit from that source, I willingly subject the validity of the preceeding narrative, and exact representation of facts, to the strictest scrutiny of the impartial and disinterested part of the community: To their equitable and candid decision therefore, this Defence of my public conduct, against all the secret arts and impotent malice of a set of invidious and plotting men, who have sought to establish their power and influence, on my injured Innocence and Reputation, is chearfully submitted.

POSTSCRIPT.

POSTSCRIPT.

†*⁎† The *Italick Letters (in parenthesis) in the Memorial to General* WASHINGTON, *were, at first, intended to point out to those parts of the Appendix, which more particularly regard the facts, there mentioned; but it being afterwards found necessary to change the order of the proofs and illustrations, the references were afterwards dropped, for the sake of connecting them with those facts, and others which were omitted in the Memorial, in the stile of a continued Narrative, for the greater ease of the Reader.*

www.ingramcontent.com/pod-product-compliance
Lightning Source LLC
Chambersburg PA
CBHW021732220426
43662CB00008B/807